SMILER REMEMBERS

SMILER REMEMBERS

Reta Wrigley

The Pentland Press
Edinburgh·Cambridge·Durham

First published in 1993 by
The Pentland Press Ltd.
1 Hutton Close
South Church
Bishop Auckland
Durham

ISBN 1 85821 082 8

Typeset by Spire Origination Ltd., Norwich
Printed and bound by Antony Rowe Ltd., Wiltshire

Foreword

Unlike our great-grandparents, most of us today take 'education' for granted. At least, we take for granted the fact that state education exists and is available for all, is free, and is compulsory up to a certain age.

Assumptions beyond that are on contentious ground, for we live in an age of rapid, and some might say, significant change. We hear of 'standard attainment tests' and 'school league tables', of 'local management of schools' and 'opting out', of 'licensed teachers', the 'the national curriculum', and the possibility of 'performance-related pay'.

It would be heartening to believe that behind these brave new phrases, the fundamental beliefs of those engaged in education remain unchanged.

So, what *is* the purpose of education?

Most replies to this question contain phrases like 'widening horizons', 'raising the sights of the child', 'independence of mind', 'the capacity to think for oneself', 'gaining skills that equip for life: literacy, numeracy, communicating, problem solving'. The focus here is on the individual and a belief in the individual's right to the opportunity to develop personal potential, talents, interests and inspirations as far as possible.

If it is the teacher's professional duty to enable this to take place, then it is no small task, and one that seems to have become more difficult in latter years.

Reta Wrigley writes from the heart, and her account of a lifetime in teaching reaches out to those of us who are feeling beset and anxious in our current educational roles. Her message is a timely reminder that we are there because of vocational calling, and that politics and bureaucracy played no part in our calling. We must stand fast by what we believe in.

Smiler Remembers is more than a personal recollection. It charts the struggle for life of a 'secondary modern' school born out of the 1944 Education Act. This was no cosy world. Resources were scarce, but the most precious resource, pupils and staff, was in place. The school's ethos, founded on 'friendliness, discipline, pride and effort' was the basis that enabled so many of its pupils to go out well equipped into the world.

The close and caring relationships described are a reminder that education does not end in the classroom. Plays, concerts, inter-school sports, educational visits, fund-raising events, social functions, are all 'voluntary' activities whereby teachers assess themselves and whereby they maintain an image of themselves as dedicated, altruistic professionals. Any withdrawal from this voluntary involvement is a very serious matter for a teaching profession today that sees itself under-valued and under attack.

Reta Wrigley's natural modesty would not allow here to see herself as a 'role model', but undoubtedly that is what she has been, and still is, to those of us fortunate to have come into contact with her.

On a very personal note, I cannot remember a time when 'Auntie Reta' did not feature in my life. As a family friend, she gave me encouragement, and this I needed in large measure as a child of eleven, one of a total of 16 pupils in a tuny rural school in one of the wilder parts of Northumberland.

For me the enormous hurdle of the 11+ loomed. Looking back, I can see that this was a turning point in my life, and held the key to my future, and subsequent entry into the teaching profession.

I know that I am not alone in believing that it was my good fortune that brought me into her ambit. I share this good fortune with all her former pupils whose activities and achievements are so lovingly recorded in this book.

Maud Isabel Warren

1.

My education began at a Dame School when I was four years old.

It was kept by an old lady named Miss Dryden. She had white hair, frizzed and piled high, and an angular but soft-skinned face. She had a neat figure and slender hands.

In the morning she always wore a long black tight-waisted dress, high at the neck, and sometimes with a narrow lace collar. She had jet beads and a watch on a chain.

In the afternoon she wore a high-necked gown of grey silk and a lace cravat stiffened with whalebone so that it reached almost up to her ears in a regal way. The jet beads were replaced by a string of pearls, but she still wore the watch.

The school was also her home. It was a double-fronted Victorian terrace house with a bay window on either side of the front door. There was a fairly long garden with a lawn, flowerbeds and one or two trees near the iron railings.

Each morning, we went in by the front entrance leaving footmarks on the sand-stoned steps, and hung our coats and hats in a little cloakroom at the right of the hall. Then we went upstairs to the schoolroom, which must originally have been a large bedroom.

There was a long table with a pale scrubbed top marked by occasional inkspots. A long backless bench extended along each side. There were two wooden chairs at the bottom and, at the top, a wooden armchair for Miss Dryden.

A coal-fire in one long wall had a bulky fireguard around it. There were white lace curtains at the windows and, I think, maps on the wall. The pupils covered a wide age range and we each sat in our appointed place at the table. The end chairs were occupied by a boy and girl who seemed, to my childish eyes, grown-up. We were expected to obey any instruction they gave us.

I cannot actually remember learning the alphabet or learning to read. Many years later I understood, Michael, the teenage boy who told me no one had taught him to read because he had always known how. That is rather how I felt myself. But I do remember learning tables by oral repetition, reciting spellings and learning to write, first by a page of slopes, then pages of hooks and, finally letters.

Good work was rewarded by a sojourn in the playroom, a smaller room at the back of the house with no furniture, but with a carpet on the floor and a good supply of toys. I vaguely remember a golliwog, an assortment of dolls, and a doll's house, but still see clearly, in my mind's eye, the rocking-horse. It was so tall it had to be mounted from a sort of platform and it had stirrups and a real mane.

The thought of riding it spurred me through the tedium of slopes and hooks, until, finally, I produced a page of well-formed letters and earned my reward. I hurried to the playroom, climbed astride the horse, grasped its neck, and set off full-speed over the hills and far away, my dark ringlets falling around my face.

The journey was short! I was lifted abruptly from my steed, my hair-ribbon adjusted, and a cold genteel voice informed me 'Ladies do not ride astride horses. Girls play with dolls.'

After that, I think the only doll I really liked was a big rag doll of my own which I sometimes smacked. I held it in real affection for quite a long time.

The mornings were given over to reading, writing and arithmetic and a general knowledge session based on a slim book of questions and answers which we had to memorise. I only remember the first question, 'Who came to England in 1066?' and the answer, 'William the Conqueror.'

In the afternoon we had music, poetry and painting. I had little draughtsman-ship, but much admired the 'works of art' produced by the older pupils – facsimile robins on twigs, an apple and an orange on a plate, and occasionally stilted flowers. My aunt, who had attended the same school eleven years earlier and had had all her formal education there, had her painted robins in a fine gilt frame on a wall at home, and I considered it a masterpiece.

We were given volumes of verse to take home some evenings to memorise, and the following day had to recite to Miss Dryden the poem which had been allotted to us.

I remember one morning before breakfast searching frantically, and without success, for my poetry book. I was much upset and afraid to go to school without it.

My father said, 'Don't worry; it will turn up. Just say, "I am very sorry, Miss Dryden, my poetry book has been mislaid but I shall bring it tomorrow!"'

I mentally rehearsed this excuse and kept trying to recall it at intervals during the day, to the detriment of whatever else I was trying to do.

Eventually the moment of confrontation came. 'Where is your poetry book, Reta?' I replied, 'I'm very sorry, Miss Dryden, I don't know, but it is something to do with a hen.'

Music lessons involved an orderly descent to the drawing-room, a rather elegant place with embossed velvet chairs and sofa, many ornaments and a piano round which we stood and sang simple songs to Miss Dryden's accompaniment.

Three o'clock was home-time, rather eagerly awaited, but marred by a ritual which preceded our departure. Each girl had a length of half-inch-wide elastic with a wooden curtain hoop attached to each end. This we had to hold behind our backs with a curtain hoop in each hand, Miss Dryden used to sit in a highbacked chair just inside her drawing-room and we each had to enter, draw our arms wide apart to extend the elastic and curtsey, saying, 'Good afternoon Miss Dryden.'

Until this had been accomplished with sufficient elegance one was not allowed to go home. I think it must have been débutante training.

When I was almost six, my parents decided to transfer me to an ordinary 'Elementary School'.

2.

Plessey Road School was built in an area of gardenless terrace houses and flats.

The Senior School was at the end of one street and the Infant and Junior School at the end of another, but the Infant School was south-west of the Senior School. They were separated by their respective schoolyards.

The Infant and Junior School had a gate near the caretaker's house and the entrance-door faced into the schoolyard. The cloakrooms were just inside the door. The lavatories were built behind a red brick wall at the opposite side of the yard, which was L shaped.

The Senior School had one entrance facing west and labelled GIRLS, and one facing south labelled BOYS. Each sex had its own walled-in playground extending in a big oblong from the entrance. There was no grass.

My first impression was of noise. I had never seen so many boys and girls *en masse* and they seemed to be moving swiftly and ruthlessly in all directions as my mother led me across the infants' playground to the school entrance.

Inside it was quiet but ugly and I became aware for the first time of the smell inimical of schools in general; a compound of disinfectant, plasticine, ink, chalk, children and general stuffiness.

There were six classrooms, more or less identical, with pinewood desks to seat two, each with a tip-up shared bench seat and an inkwell in a socket to each half desk. Each room had a teacher's desk with a high wooden chair on a dais, and a line of shiny stained wooden cupboards. The window sills were high so we could not look out at the flats on the other side of the cobbled street. Walls and ceilings were drab. For many years brown dadoes and green walls seemed uniform in schools, I remember with what pleasure we selected light bright colour schemes when teachers were eventually allowed a choice.

The Headmistress had a large knee-hole desk on a dais in one of the rooms, but no private room of her own. She usually taught the top class herself.

5

My mother conversed with her on that first morning, apparently giving her information she required, and then went away, leaving me feeling very small in a large bleak place.

The Headmistress, a rather forbidding person, tall, angular and neat, handed me over to a teacher in one classroom and then rang a handbell. Silence descended outside and the children marched in, line by line, each class supervised by a teacher. They took their places behind their desks, I was shown to an empty space, and we were told to put our hands together and say the Lord's Prayer. This was followed by a lengthy roll call and a Bible story.

Next came Tables practice and Arithmetic. I knew my tables and found the simple sums easy. The teacher took me to the Headmistress who passed a book to me, and told me to open it anywhere and read to her. This was my introduction to *Hiawatha*.

I was transferred at once to the Headmistress's class where I was, I think, a year younger than anyone else, so the groundwork at the Dame School had apparently been sound.

I found the manner of working very boring. All reading was done aloud, by rote, a paragraph per person. It was tedious and, to me, impossible to wait for each stumbling and expressionless performer, I was always pages ahead when it came to my turn and, I was reprimanded constantly for not 'keeping the place.'

I liked problems but hated mechanical arithmetic which seemed pointless.

We had History and Geography lessons where the teacher talked a lot and sometimes banged a stick on the blackboard to command attention. I daydreamed a lot.

I hated 'plasticine' lessons which took place on two afternoons a week. We were each given a dirty board of a nondescript colour, a wad of mixed green and red clay and a little spatula. We were told to make a variety of objects. I only remember one enjoyable afternoon when I made a Hiawatha scene with little wigwams in it. I loathed the feel and smell of old plasticine.

The girls embroidered hessian bags with thick coloured wools and learnt to knit, making cotton dishcloths on thick wooden needles, whilst the boys practised drawing lines, angles and shapes with a ruler and pencil.

We used slates for sums and sentences, and the sound of squeaky slate pencils made my spine tingle. We used to bring pieces of rag from home with which to clean our slates, vigorous rubbing assisted by a bit of surreptitious spit.

It was sad having to eradicate a piece of work which one liked.

The rooms looked better in summer because we used to gather cowslips and buttercups in the meadows and take them to the teacher who used to put them in jam jars on the high window-sills.

After the genteel atmosphere of Miss Dryden's the playground seemed turbulent and boisterous. The boys used to pull their jersey sleeves over their hands and run around in random directions pretending to be monkeys and frightening girls.

We all played hide-and-seek, and song-and-rhyme games, but I never minded when the bell rang and it was time to go back into school; I didn't like noise and confusion.

Once we were all abruptly sent home for a few months as soldiers were billeted in the two school buildings before going to France. I remember going with my mother in the mornings, carrying cans of tea and cakes or sandwiches to hand through the railings to a soldier. All the local people did this, their tribute, I suppose, to the men so soon to be in the battle-line.

I remember the long columns of marching khaki-clad troops and the jingling of the cavalry horse-harnesses the night they went away, men of the Northumberland Fusiliers and Durham Light Infantry, the majority of whom were killed on the battlefields of France.

In due course, the 'Top Class' was transferred across the schoolyard to the 'Big School' as the Senior Department was known.

Here, there was a Headmaster, named Acquila Foster, and several male teachers as well as female.

Classrooms opened out on three sides of an oblong central hall, which was itself divided across the centre by a moveable glass partition to make two temporary classrooms used for music and 'drill' (Physical Exercises).

Each morning the school assembled in the hall, in lines on either side of the partition, marching in to a tune played on the piano by a plump pretty teacher with red hair. The Headmaster conducted the assembly, prayers, hymn-singing and general reprimanding, from the open end of the partition. He shouted most of the time, often seemed to lose his temper, disapproved of the smallest unauthorised movement or whisper, and banged on the glass with his cane to emphasise his points. Sometimes, he did this so vigorously he broke a pane. I was afraid of him and longed for assembly to be over and the orderly march to classrooms completed. He banged his stick to emphasise the beat of the march.

He was a quick-tempered man, but not unkind, as I discovered some years later when I was in the top class and taught mostly by him. He was strict; work had to be done thoroughly and in silence. He was never conversational with a class, but was interested in the progress of his pupils.

Sometimes, from my first entering the school, a teacher would send me to him to show him a composition I had written. He would praise the work, and occasionally read it to his class, much to my embarrassment. I still have the testimonial he wrote for me years later when I was applying for entrance to a Teacher Training College.

I enjoyed writing compositions, reading, and was interested enough in Arithmetic, feeling some pride if all mechanical examples were correct, and enjoying with my imagination problems where trains passed each other in opposite directions and at varying speeds, or baths filled and emptied at different speeds. Later, I found Algebra interesting again because imagination could regard the mysterious x in so many ways.

'English Exercises' from set primers were extremely boring and memories of my early experience made me ban them almost entirely from my own syllabus when I became an English teacher.

I recognise the use of knowing how to parse and analyse sentences but the way in which it was used as a daily exercise was tedious. I always remember one example:- ''Parse and analyse, 'Gather ye rosebuds while ye may' ''. We were not given enough time to 'gather the rosebuds'.

As a teacher, allocations of money were spent on lots of books to read and enjoy, instead of on sets of primers. I also made sure everyone had ample time to finish reading a chosen book, having regard to the unsatisfactory 'library lessons' at Plessey Road School. These were twenty minute periods when we chose, or scrambled for, one of an assortment of books in a cupboard. I could become engrossed in any book, but they were all collected at the end of the lesson, and, however much I pushed and wriggled, I seldom got the book I had begun the week before. It was like reading several serial stories simultaneously and I had left the school before I really found out 'What Katy Did'.

I must have been a most exasperating child so far as the Needlework teacher was concerned. She was elderly, severe and old-fashioned, but I truly made no effort. We provided our own material for whatever garment we were supposed to make. I can't remember completing anything, and seemed to spend most of my time 'stroking gathers'. This seemed a completely pointless exercise and I used to read *The School Friend* concealed on my knees, as I scratched away with a needle at the tiny folds. Once I was caned for doing this and felt an unjustifiable resentment.

One morning each week was spent at a Domestic Science Centre in an old building, Forster Board School, at the other end of the town, and I enjoyed this outing.

It was pleasurable to walk through the town in schooltime; missing the forbidding assembly; looking fleetingly in shops and at market stalls on the way.

By modern standards, the Cookery Room was poorly appointed, but we took our own ingredients and made something edible each week. Usually, we took home whatever we had made, apart from surreptitious sampling, but occasionally we cooked a dinner and ate it at the Centre, after setting the 'dining table' (a scrubbed wooden bench) appropriately.

My mother had encouraged me to help her to cook from a very early age; punching dough, rolling pastry with a miniature rolling-pin on a specially made little board, making treacle toffee, spice buns and gingerbread, so I managed my school cookery with ease.

Whilst we attended the Domestic Science Centre, the boys went to school allotments near the Spartans Football Field, escorted by a weak and harassed master. They took a long time to reach their destination, carrying their tools with them and engaging in considerable horseplay and tomfoolery before they settled to their appointed tasks. Consequently, little real gardening was done and the allotments were not very productive.

History and Geography comprised reading in turn from text books, looking at atlases hung on the blackboard and memorising significant dates. I contributed little interest or concentration only recalling with pleasure a Geography lesson given by a temporary teacher. She took us on an imaginary journey across Canada from east to west and I have never forgotten the scenery conjured up by her description and by the pictures she showed us.

Eventually, I sat and passed what was then known as 'the scholarship examination' and progressed to the local place of higher education, Blyth Secondary School.

3.

This was a long two-storeyed building divided into two sections, one for girls and one for boys. We shared a central hall-cum-gymnasium on the ground level and Art and Science rooms on the floor above, but never had co-educational classes. Our respective playing-fields, behind the school, were separated by a tall wooden fence. The girls' tennis and netball courts were to the left of the building, the boys' tennis courts and general playing area to the right. In front of the school was a lawn with flower beds and this was forbidden territory for everyone. Any friendly encounters between the sexes were clandestine.

For the first time I needed a school uniform; navy blue serge gym-tunic (knee-length) white blouses, red ties, and black stockings. A hat was also compulsory, cream straw with a red and white school band in summer and a small navy cloth cap piped with red in winter. Prefects could wear skirts instead of gym-slips, but elaborate hair styles and permanent-waving were forbidden, also any form of jewellery except a school badge. Long hair had to be tied back with a plain red ribbon, and when I arrived one morning wearing a velvet ribbon I was unobtrusively drawn aside by the Headmistress and requested not to wear velvet again.

On arrival at school we had to change into white gym shoes. Calf-length buttoned boots were in vogue then and I well remember the struggles I had with a button-hook at our brief lunch break, changing to go home. I often went with every odd button undone. Worst of all was forgetting or losing one's button-hook; fastening tiny leather buttons with fingers alone is a long and tedious business. Button-hooks were prized possessions, made of steel but with ornamental handles of wood, bone or tortoiseshell.

I don't think anyone felt really rebellious about wearing school uniform, although we did grumble on hot summer days when we longed for cotton frocks and short socks instead of serge gym-slips and black woollen stockings.

11

English lessons now became a delight. We had a lively intelligent teácher, Miss Farrer, with a sense of humour and a love of literature. There was a good library. We were encouraged to read and to write, to be critical and to use imagination. We read and discussed poetry, plays, novels (classical and modern) and books of essays, assessing content and style. We were given a diversity of themes to stretch imagination and extend vocabulary. One title, *Luck's Cavern* enabled me to write a short story when I was fifteen which was published shortly afterwards in a northern weekly magazine. The acceptance slip and a postal order for five shillings (25p) marked my first venture into print.

I also discovered that History is not just a matter of dates, rulers and battles, but is the story of humankind and the effect of environment and circumstances on people. I began to search through local records, in the Reference Room at the Public Library, linking up local happenings to their place and significance in national and world affairs.

By means of this pastime I gained information which enabled me to write short articles with a topical link for the weekend literary page of the *Newcastle Weekly Chronicle*.

I wish I had realized that Geography has the same significance. Instead, it was to me a boring memorization of places, rivers, products, rainbelts and trade winds. It was only when I came to realise the significance of Physical Geography in shaping the lives of people that I became interested. But I read travel books and took imaginary journeys all over the world.

The only subject I really hated was Art, even though I have always had an innate love of colour and design, form and texture, and have always been aware of these in nature. But Art was still the copying of objects. Attempts were made to teach perspective and art forms but always with a vase, bottle, jug or some such object on a low table in the centre of the oval of desks in the Art Room. I used to try to get a seat where I couldn't see the handle, if there was one, and therefore wouldn't have to draw it, I shaded with a soft pencil without having any idea why.

Even worse was having to copy, from a card, intricate geometric designs to scale, yet I could have enjoyed composing a design of my own. I should have loved Art as it is taught now, with scope for free expression, colour and imagination. I regularly visit a local First School in a very old-fashioned building with a high oblong central hall. But the walls, from floor to ceiling, are filled with friezes done as projects, every child participating. In spring there are lambs, buds, eggs, daffodils, primroses against bold green and blue backgrounds. The scenes change according to season and topical circumstance.

The Queen's Jubilee display was magnificent and amusing. One picture portrayed her visit to Tonga. Except for the Queen's (which was bright pink) every face, including the Duke of Edinburgh's was painted brown.

The Christmas show is best of all with angels, shepherds, carol singers, reindeers, Santas, decorated trees, presents, around all four walls and each child's individual dangling tinsel-and-silver expression of joy suspended from the roof. But Art was joyless at Blyth Secondary School.

Miss Murdoch, an intelligent intellectual Scotswoman was Headmistress. She had a true sense of vocation; she was a firm disciplinarian, but just and understanding in most circumstances. She taught Latin herself.

She demonstrated how a school can be a community as well as a place of learning. We had a debating society, a school choir, and occasional school journeys. There were school concerts and inter-house competitions in Games and Athletics. We each, I think, felt a part of the whole.

I had no athletic ability but enjoyed participating.

Eventually, I gained a School Certificate in numerous subjects and afterwards good results in English, History and French at an Advanced level.

Thus academically equipped, I discarded gym slips for the rather shapeless clothes of the time, put my hair up in earphones (a coil of plaits over each ear) and departed to Hull Municipal Training College.

I had accepted my father's advice that it was better to have a career with a regular income and then write as I chose, than to enter the competition of journalism and write as directed by people whose opinions and attitudes I might not always be able to share or to respect.

4.

In retrospect, and considering the freedom demanded by students today, I am astounded that we accepted the college rules and regulations as meekly as we did.

Every student had to be in college no later than six o'clock, Monday to Friday, and by eight o'clock on Saturday and Sunday. No visitors were allowed without permission from the Principal and this was not freely given. Even then they could only be entertained in the common room and during the afternoon. No male visitors were permitted at any time except on the two official Open Days when fathers could be escorted round the building.

A cup of cocoa and a slice of bread and butter could be had in the refectory at nine o'clock after which each student was expected to return to her room to prepare for bed, the lights-out bell sounding at ten-thirty.

The rising-bell went at seven o'clock and each student had to be seated at her appointed table in the refectory by eight o'clock to partake of breakfast after having sung grace in Latin. The Latin Benedictus preceded and followed each formal meal of the day.

Food was plain, substantial and meagre in quantity; fish appeared with sickening monotony – it was cheap in Hull.

The home of my erstwhile Maths teacher at Blyth was in Hull. She wrote to tell me she was coming home for a weekend and would like me to have tea with her family on the Saturday and go to the theatre afterwards to see a classical play.

I sought permission to accept the invitation but was told by the Tutor in Residence that I might go to tea and stay until nine o'clock as a special favour but the theatre visit could not be allowed as I would not get back to college before lights out at ten-thirty.

The only evening performance I ever saw at the Theatre Royal was when Sybil Thorndyke appeared in a new production there. She was a friend of the Principal and we went *en masse*.

Next morning, she visited the college, talked to us in assembly, and signed autographs. It was a memorable occasion, for she had a beautiful rich deep voice and a magnificent presence.

To go anywhere hatless was forbidden.

Birthdays were celebrated by surreptitious gatherings of a few friends in one's room for a slice of cake and a glass of sherry or port, strictly against the rules.

My greatest frustration was over 'teaching practice' when we spent three or four weeks each term teaching in one of the city schools, closely observed by college tutors.

I knew positively I intended to teach Seniors when I qualified, pupils in the eleven to sixteen group and I made this quite clear whenever I was interviewed or filled in a form. But because I am only five feet tall and slightly built, everyone assumed I would be unable to control older pupils and should teach Infants. This advice I constantly rejected and consequently found myself allocated to the youngest classes in Junior schools. My time was half over before I had the opportunity to teach even thirteen year-olds. Then I was sent, I think deliberately to prove me wrong, to a boys' school in a rough part of the city.

There I had a successful session: no problems with discipline, good reports for lesson presentation and content, but with one reprimand. On school practice we had to wear plain long-sleeved overalls over our normal clothing. To teach Games and P.E. we had to wear our knee-length black gym tunics, cream blouses and black woollen stockings. One afternoon, thus clad at the end of a Games session, I walked into the Staff Room, containing MEN, without first donning my overall, a most depraved action for which I was duly censured.

I taught Physical Education badly, especially when I was being watched, as I felt self-conscious and confused. Other subjects, with the exception of English and History which were always highly commended, received mediocre reports. I think the Staff thought I might just manage to be an average teacher and my final report was passable but not enthusiastic.

However, I did edit the college magazine, quite a literary publication, and wrote a short story *L'Envoi* for it which earned unexpected praise from the Principal.

There was a good library and I spent hours reading widely, huddled by the radiator in my room in winter, lying on the grass in summer among buttercups in the long meadow in which the hostel stood. I recall insects whirring, church bells chiming at intervals, warmth, peace, leisure and books.

After two years it was over. Goodbyes were said without reluctance and I returned home gladly with piles of conflicting notes on teaching method and child psychology, to apply for a post as a teacher.

5.

My first teaching post was in an All-Standard School rather like the Elementary School I had myself attended, but the building was a little more modern. It was E shaped.

The long end comprised a central hall flanked by three classrooms. The little centre arm housed Practical rooms – Domestic Science and Woodwork. There were six classrooms along each end arm. The Staff room and Head teacher's room were up a flight of stairs at the end of each short arm, above the cloakrooms.

The Infant school, with a separate Head and Staff, occupied the eastern part of the building, the combined Junior and Senior school the west, that is the hall, practical rooms and nine classrooms.

There were netball courts in winter and tennis courts in summer in between the arms of the E and these were the girls' playing areas exclusively. The Infants had a long playground at the east end, the boys a similar one at the west. There was no playing field and the boys had to go to a municipal pitch for cricket and football.

I entered this building in August 1930, feeling very shy, inadequate and inexperienced, for my first days as a qualified teacher.

The Headmaster gave me a syllabus of subjects, a work record book in which to make preparatory notes for lessons, a timetable, and a register for Form 1A. Then he led me into a small classroom filled with desks, and ten minutes later, with children, sixty of them, boys and girls about equal in number, all eyeing me curiously and weighing me up.

I recall my blushing consternation and a feeling that I knew nothing at all about teaching. We said the Lord's Prayer and after that I heard my own voice, sounding like that of a stranger, calling out the name of each child on the register. Then began the daily routine: mental arithmetic; spellings; sums;

reading; drawing (again selected objects detailed in the syllabus); History and Geography (dull set lessons from dull text books, and I did not immediately recognise how I could extend the lessons beyond these dull limits).

I used to struggle home each evening with sixty English exercise books and sixty Arithmetic books to check, after staying late to mark sixty drawn objects.

My class seemed at first just a sea of faces and a surge of ebbing and flowing sound. If it 'flowed' much, the Headmaster was in the habit of pouncing into the room, yelling at the children and informing me that I must keep the children quiet at all times.

One afternoon, in my second week, he found me walking around the desks marking drawings as children completed them and he lectured me loudly on my laziness.

I grew more anxious each day and lost all confidence in my ability. I was afraid to mention my fears to other members of the staff because I felt so inferior, and was determined not to show my feelings at home because my parents would have been so disappointed.

Then came the day I made an error in marking the register. The register ritual in schools was an absurdity: the calling out of each child's name in alphabetical order; each child's individual 'Yes Miss'; a stroke for each one present, an 0 for each absentee; the total number present inserted in a square at the foot of the page. Some teachers made the class sit in silence, each child either with hands on head or arms folded, until the ritual was completed.

In my room was a buzz of sound. Someone replied in place of an absentee; I put a stroke instead of an 0 and also had to alter the total at the bottom. Then, as was customary, I sent the register to the Headmaster's room.

Shortly afterwards, he slung open the classroom door, ordered my class to join that of another teacher in the hall, and said to me, 'You go to my room!'

When he joined me there, he gave me a lecture on the necessity to mark registers with accuracy, to prepare lesson notes fully and always to take all marking home. He said he had known my grandparents and they would have been most disappointed at my laziness and ineptitude, and that if I marked a register wrongly again I could lose my job. As it was, I must sign the log book, acknowledging my error. This I did with a trembling hand and returned to my room feeling like an outcast with no future to look forward to.

Marking a register became a nightmare, I did it faintly in pencil, checked, and went over it in ink. I felt a failure and used to cycle to Plessey Woods occasionally on a Saturday to weep where no one could see me.

Then at the end of term the Headmaster retired. How thankfully I contributed towards his leaving present.

After Christmas came a new and smiling Head. I found I was liking the children and they were liking me. I relaxed. Things improved.

Until the afternoon when a boy answered the register in the wrong order; the stroke was in, instead of the 0, in ink!

Consternation! This is the end, I thought. With pounding heart, I climbed the stairs, register in hand, and knocked on the Headmaster's door.

Entering when bidden, I blurted out, 'I've made a mistake'.

He looked at me quizzically, without speaking, opened a drawer of his desk, and produced a cane. 'Which hand will you have it on?' he asked, with a smile.

My relief was immense, I poured out the tale of my errors and inadequacies.

He was most kind; told me teachers made mistakes at times and that I should never have signed the log book; that my relationship with the class was good and that I worked, if anything, too hard.

I was able to settle down and enjoy teaching from that moment.

I never called names again, but merely counted the number of children present and looked to see which individuals, if any, were absent, then marked the register accordingly. It was a simple clerical procedure. But all my teaching life afterwards I was noted for my neat and accurate registers. No one wished to mark mine if I was away from school in case its appearance was spoilt.

Gradually school numbers increased and it was necessary to have two classes in the hall, one facing east, the other west, with a gap of about two yards between, I was given a class of sixty-two nine-year-olds at one end, an elderly woman teacher sixty-one at the other. She was kind to me in a patronizing way.

She used to sit and embroider little mats whilst her class chanted spellings and tables aloud and I tried to hold the attention of my class.

She decided we should share the first half hour of the day, devoted to hymn-singing and a Bible story, taking charge on alternate days. When it was her turn, the period began, whatever the weather or season, with a full-throated rendering of *Summer suns are glowing over land and sea.*

When it was my turn she usually left me to it and went to the Staff Room. If she had a headache, which seemed to happen rather frequently, she stayed there quite a long time. So I conducted hymn-singing, told a Bible-story, then did spellings, tables and mental arithmetic with one hundred and twenty three nine-year-olds. It was excellent training in class-control; I never felt overwhelmed by numbers afterwards.

Enforcing discipline, especially of the orderly, subdued nature demanded in those days, was not easy. It required strong will-power, mutual understanding and, occasionally, punishment.

One morning a small boy in the other class was fooling about, and tumult was approaching. After several warnings, I went across and slammed a ruler down on his knuckles as he was raising them to do battle with a willing neighbour. The surprise attack nonplussed him, order was restored and work proceeded.

In the afternoon his father came to complain because I had punished Billy and he was not in my class. But having surveyed the scene, he commiserated with me, warned his son, and left in friendly fashion.

Billy became a butcher and, forty-eight years later, has his own business. Four years ago, at an Adult Association dance, a little, balding man with a cheerful face came over and invited me to dance. It was Billy. He told me who he was and introduced me to his wife, telling her he had recognised me at once as I looked 'just the same'. She and I smiled at one another, each aware of my grey hair and wrinkles. Pupils of bygone years have said this to me so often that I have decided all we really notice is a familiar expression, or maybe a basically unchanging personality.

The new Headmaster, Mr. Lisle, decided to introduce specialization in some subjects, a new trend in elementary teaching. He did not consider special aptitudes but just allocated subjects, so I found myself teaching so-called 'General Science' to four classes.

The syllabus, which one was expected to follow slavishly, was just a list e.g. china; glass; salt; pepper; sun; moon.

Despite initial dismay, this work proved interesting to me and to the children, as it was easy to link with local history. For instance, salt from pans near Blyth Harbour had been taken by sailing ships to London for its citizens to use in preserving meat. Monks of Newminster Abbey, near Morpeth, had owned one such pan and swapped salt for tuns of wine from London wine merchants.

Glass proved a particularly interesting topic as there had been a glass works on the outskirts of Blyth and three at Seaton Sluice, a village three miles away, from the eighteenth century until about a hundred years ago. They made bottles chiefly, but also some ornaments, and work people used to make glass balls for their children's Christmas trees. I still have two, a silvery one made for my grandmother and a green one made for my father. I showed these at school, children talked about them at home and soon were bringing similar things owned by their grandparents. If time had permitted it would have made a valuable class project, but timetables had to be rigidly adhered to and General Science lessons were brief.

I had to teach Needlework and Knitting too, and for this stroking gathers had not equipped me very well. Two classes of girls joined for these subjects whilst the boys 'did Plasticine' with another teacher.

I had sixty-seven nine-year-old girls, each expected, according to the syllabus, to knit an egg cosy on four needles and sew a pair of pilch knickers after I had cut them out. With one pair of very stiff cutting-out scissors and the help of the teacher who supervised the boys and their plasticine, I spent lunch hours cutting out sixty-seven pairs of white cotton pilch knickers (now called briefs).

In knitting periods the girls spent an hour tangling wool on four needles. Then I used to take the tangles home. My mother untangled them, cast on again and knitted a little of each ready for me to take back to be retangled the following lesson. Eventually, I think she completed sixty-seven egg cosies.

I always remember one little girl, Jean, who would today have attended a special E.S.N. school. I gave her two thick wooden needles and a ball of thick coloured wool to tangle, and to do this she used to stand in the big waste-paper basket, which, for some reason was a favourite place of hers. Poor child, she was burnt to death a year later when her winceyette nightgown caught fire.

At the end of each scholastic year, the Headmaster wrote a criticism of a teacher's ability in each subject, but the Needlework report was written by the Senior Mistress. From her I received the only wholly adverse criticism I have ever had. It was succinct.

'The Needlework produced by this class is not up to the required standard'.

Probably perfectly true, but I did think she might have mitigated the censure by mentioning the size of the class. Now twenty is regarded as the maximum number for any class engaged in practical work.

The classes were large, the syllabuses constricted, the discipline strict, books and apparatus in short supply, yet my recollection is of happy, well-adjusted children.

Naturally, there was mischief and some misbehaviour with classes so large in such small rooms. Occasionally my patience was exhausted.

One morning, the class had grown quite unruly and I told them I thought I must buy a cane. At playtime, Robert, a tall rangy lad with rosy cheeks and a big smile, asked if he could fetch a cane for me during the lunch hour. I gave him the necessary sixpence (2$^1/_2$p).

In the afternoon, he came in swishing a long thin cane and handed it over to me. I hung it on the end of the blackboard and the sight of it seemed to have a salutary effect. In fact, there was an unnatural quiet, except for Robert. He behaved so badly, paid no heed to either entreaties or threats, until eventually I said, "Well, I must cane *you*, Robert."

He came to me, held out his hand, and I administered the threatened punishment with a heavy heart and insufficient athletic ability. He gave me a kind slow smile, said, 'I just wanted to find out if I'd got you a good one,' and sat down satisfied.

His father, a widower, owned greyhounds and Robert used to tell me which dog to put my money on. I never admitted I didn't try to profit from his tips.

After a time, his father married again, this time to a Roman Catholic. Robert came to school and informed me rather sadly that he was 'turning Catholic' and would have to transfer to the Catholic School at the end of the month.

I said, 'If your father wishes, you can leave at the end of the week.'

'No' he replied, 'I'm not turning till the end of the month.'

Some years later at a dance, I met a Regimental Sergeant Major in full uniform, in one of those 'Excuse me' waltzes, where you dance with whoever you meet when the music pauses.

He talked as if he knew me and then said rather reproachfully, 'I don't think you know who I am.' When I admitted I didn't, he said, 'I'm Robert.'

I should have recognised the rosy cheeks and laughing eyes even though his moustache rather muzzled the smile.

I still meet some of the boys and girls of those early teaching days. One boy became a doctor, one a naval architect.

Whilst under a dryer at the hairdresser's recently, someone under the next one said, 'You used to be Miss Mitcheson, didn't you?' I said, 'Yes.' She said, 'I recognised you as you came in. You taught me at Princess Louise Road School when I was a little girl.'

After reminiscing about those far-off days for a while she talked about her grandchildren.

A month ago as I was about to alight from a bus, the burly grey-haired driver said, 'Remember me, Miss Mitcheson? You taught me at P.L.R. school.'

Then all the passengers had to wait, somewhat to my embarrassment, whilst he recalled how I had comforted him and restored his confidence when he arrived very late, and consequently fearful, on a snowy morning.

Pleasant encounters which occur from time to time to recall memories of my earliest teaching days.

6.

In 1932, there was a Government-decreed reorganisation of education and the Secondary Modern School came into being, the much-maligned eleven-plus examination replacing the old scholarship examination which had not been compulsory.

This resulted in three educational age-groups: Infants 5 to 7+. Juniors 7+ to 11, Secondary Modern 11+ to 14 or Grammar 11+ to 16 or 18.

A new Infant School was built and our building made into a Secondary Modern School, the girls occupying the old Infant section and the boys the part where I had taught. Practical rooms were extended and refitted as Domestic Science, Woodwork and Metalwork rooms. A classroom at each end was altered and equipped as a Science Laboratory.

All the women on the Staff were moved to the Girls' Secondary Modern School under a Headmistress and the men stayed on with the boys and current Headmaster.

The seven years that followed were easy and happy. We were a united friendly Staff, mostly young, and we had a perfect Headmistress, Miss Nan Wilson, motherly, compassionate and herself an excellent teacher. She guided us unobtrusively, was interested in each one of us personally, and was held in affectionate regard by all the girls.

I believe in co-education; it is natural for the sexes to mingle, but teaching boys and girls separately is less demanding. Mixed, they show off for one another; it is a form of display like birds and other creatures at mating-times. Taught separately they compete to please a teacher, to shine individually, and a self-disciplined class is the norm.

There was almost total specialization, so I spent almost all my days teaching English. I was able to plan my own scheme of work. I ordered as wide a variety of books as finance allowed: fiction; travel; biography; poetry. The girls read them, talked about them, occasionally wrote about them and we examined the use of words. Everyone built up an anthology of poetry, which she illustrated with drawings or cut-out pictures and gradually girls began writing poetry.

They were encouraged to use imagination, delight in words, and enjoy writing stories, essays and letters. Their most pleasing work they transcribed and illustrated. This was supposed to represent their manuscript appearing in print. On leaving school they took their original work and poetry anthologies with them, and I meet past pupils who still treasure these books and show them with pride to their own children.

The girls were friendly but respectful: interested in what the teachers wore, how they looked, and how they spent their private lives, but they were not inquisitive or impertinent.

I well remember the Monday morning I arrived newly-engaged, wearing an emerald ring and feeling decidedly self-conscious. It was a morning of whispers, nudges, smiles and general excitement.

Woolworths must have sold more rings set with green stones the following week than was customary. Their appearance made me realize, as I have done many times since, how important the influence of a teacher's appearance can be.

Some months later, I lost an emerald and the ring had to be returned to the jeweller for repair. I had been feeding a little Shetland pony in a field when it grabbed my coat sleeve. I tried to pull my arm away and it transferred its teeth to my ring, swallowed an emerald and crushed part of the claw setting, so the repair was intricate and needed time. I had to appear at school without it.

There was immediate covert consternation, whispers, stares, sad expressions, general dolour, until I said, 'It is all right, I'm still engaged, just not wearing a ring.'

I told them the story, and after the ensuing relief and amusement, we were able to settle peacefully to work.

The Headmistress encouraged school excursions to places of interest in the county and we sometimes took parties of girls to the Theatre Royal at Newcastle.

One small group of particularly intelligent girls stayed on at school after the statutory leaving age of fourteen. They showed a definite interest in literature, including Shakespeare, so we used to go to Saturday matinees to see Donald Wolfitt in *Macbeth* or *Hamlet* and afterwards have tea together in the café of a department store.

The atmosphere was one of genial scholarship, but the physical side of education was also encouraged. There was no gymnasium and no playing-field, but able, dedicated teaching made up for lack of facilities, and trophies adorning the corridor marked the girls success in inter-school competitions.

Some of the friendliness I experienced at Princess Louise Road Girls' Secondary Modern School has lasted through many years. In 1979, my husband and I celebrated our Ruby Wedding Anniversary, and among the thirty-five guests were two people I had taught all those years ago, Mary Graham with her husband Alan, and Elsie Crozier with her husband, two sons and daughter. Their second son, Andrew, is our godson.

September, 1939 saw the outbreak of the Second World War. My fiancé was likely to be called up at any moment, so we decided to be married in October. Married women were not allowed to teach except as temporary 'stand-ins' for absentees, so I submitted my resignation. I left at the end of September, laden with presents and bouquets, after bidding farewell to my loyal, affectionate and somewhat tearful pupils.

7.

During the next year I did brief spells of supply-teaching in a wide range of schools, including three months with six-year-olds in an Infant School.

This was a new and interesting experience and I learnt quite a lot, though to what extent the little ones benefited is less certain.

I loved 'story' lessons, when they all gathered round with eager faces, on which changing expressions reflected the mood of the story. They loved simple stories which I made up as I went along. The trouble was they always asked for the same story again at a later date, by which time little details had gone from my mind. Such errors and omissions were corrected by them with a mixture of eagerness and scorn.

We had whole afternoons with poster colours, chalks, paste, and all kinds of bits and pieces, doing 'handwork'.

I learnt that one draws an apple or an orange by starting with a faint dot of the correct colour in the middle and colouring round and round it until the right shape is reached. This was after the Headmistress found me struggling to teach them how to drawn an outline for an apple. My drawing ability improved a little.

We made rocking horses with halves of circular cheese boxes for the rockers. I had to cut out eighty 'outline' horses in thin cardboard, two for each child. They coloured them, put in identifying features, glued the heads, bodies and tails together, and then the legs were fastened to the half cheese box.

I disliked mixing the regulation tapwater paste as it easily became lumpy, so I bought a large tin of Gripfix. I turned around one afternoon to find a little boy eating it from the tin using the brush as a spoon, with apparent enjoyment.

We had messy, colourful, enthusiastic sessions. How far removed from the grubby, smelly plasticine 'handwork' lessons of my own childhood.

It was a time of air-raids and if the sirens sounded during the night, people moved into their air-raid shelters until the 'all-clear' sounded. Consequently, children were often too tired to come to school next morning.

After one such occasion, a sturdy mischievous little boy with fair curly hair did not come to school until the afternoon.

He said, 'We had a lovely time in our shelter last night, miss. We had a little stove and my mam made tea and bacon sandwiches, and it was nice and warm.'

I said, 'That was nice, Roger, I had no stove in my shelter and I was cold. I think the next time the sirens go, I'll come to your shelter.'

He sat down with dampened ardour, looking rather nonplussed.

After a while he came forward, gave my skirt a tug, to attract attention, and said, 'Miss! If you got yourself a candle and put it in a plant pot you'd be warm enough in your own shelter.'

One morning the sirens wailed during lesson-time and we shepherded all the little ones into the long bleak school shelters with their bare brick walls and slatted wooden benches.

There they sat enthusiastically singing of their own accord. 'Roll out the Barrel' and 'We'll hang out the washing on the Siegfried line'.

The irony was that the enemy had already penetrated the Maginot Line in France.

At the end of term I was transferred elsewhere. As I bade her goodbye, the Headmistress said she was sorry I had not trained to be an Infant teacher as I had the right attitude. I did not share her regret though I recall my brief stay in her school with affection.

As male teachers were increasingly called to serve in the Armed Forces, more work became available to supply teachers on a long-term basis. As their relevant age-group was announced all unemployed women had to sign-on at the local Labour Exchange and were detailed for public service of some sort. Women teachers had to replace men. I was sent to Princess Louise Road Secondary Modern Boys' School, the other half of the school building where I had so happily taught girls.

I found myself the only woman teacher on an otherwise all-male Staff and made a rather bashful appearance the first morning.

However, I received a friendly welcome and found I was to teach English mainly. The man I was replacing had a similar approach to the subject as I had, so the syllabus presented no problems.

I was something of a novelty to the boys and they were mostly anxious to please me. It was then I discovered the advantage of being only five feet tall.

Most of them were taller than me and tended to be protective rather than aggressive.

I had intended to go to the Staffroom at the other end of the school when coffee-break time arrived, but discovered the men had bought a teapot now there was an excuse for cups of tea. So I just became part of the male staff and was joined a couple of months later by two other women teachers.

I had a happy time there until April 1942 when I received a note from the Education Office telling me to report the following Monday at New Delaval Secondary Modern School, the school at which my husband had taught until he joined the RAF in December, 1940.

8.

It is difficult to decide how to begin writing about my life at this school where I eventually taught for more than twenty years.

I am surrounded by mementoes of those happy years; oak candlesticks on the mantelpiece, a handmade wooden bowl with an inlaid panel on my desk, a picture on a wall, the pale green glass vase with roses in it on the bookcase; brass ornaments and corn dollies in the hall, cruets and a lemon squeezer in the kitchen, a crocheted hat and scarf in my favourite colours, my needlecase with a verse about friendship on it; the mother-of-pearl fish brooch pinned to my lapel; a bottle of liqueur brandy brought recently by a boy I taught many years ago – to name but a few.

Or there are photographs and snapshots, taken over the years, which if put in sequence would tell the story of my life, I think, helped by letters and cards received from various places in the world. They still arrive, especially at Christmas, and it is warming to know that past pupils remember me as, indeed, I remember them.

I think before I begin, as I suppose one should, at the beginning, I'll tell you about three of those presents, as they epitomise the relationship we enjoyed.

The children in the early forties, like those of today, used to go round the doors in the weeks preceding Christmas singing carols and collecting money. My class of fourteen-year-olds had been spending their evenings in this way, including singing outside the houses of members of the Staff, but had never visited me, although they had asked me to name my favourite carol.

Knowing it was the one they most enjoyed singing, I had said, '*While shepherds watched* with a descant.'

The end of term came and I still hadn't been serenaded by *While shepherds watched*, which rather puzzled me.

Then on Christmas Eve I heard it. I opened the door and there they all were, singing their carol and holding out a parcel. It contained a card signed by each of them, and the oak candlesticks.

I invited them in to have homemade ginger wine and biscuits, and, in the course of conversation, discovered they had used their carol-singing money to buy the candlesticks.

I received my mother-of-pearl fish brooch in its gilt setting a year before I retired from teaching.

The Art Master was due to leave at the end of the summer term and classes were collecting money for a leaving-present. My form of fifteen-sixteen year-olds seemed to empty their box to count the money every morning as I marked the register.

Eventually, I said, 'Shall I keep the box in my desk for you until you need it?'

I never counted the money personally, but they opened the tin regularly to drop in contributions.

When the time came to purchase the present they retrieved the tin and began to argue about what to buy for the Art Master. I thought they had collected a considerable sum and tried to help with suggestions such as motoring or gardening accessories. A girl said, 'Oh, we haven't enough money to buy anything like that for him.'

I said, 'I'm sure you must have; the tin was heavy enough.'

The last day of term came and I went into an unusually silent classroom, and found a little box on my desk. It contained the fish.

That was what they had been saving for. In a Religious Education lesson I had told them about seeing the sign of the fish in the Catacombs in Rome and that had given them the idea when they looked in the window of a local jeweller's shop.

The third gift is one of my most treasured possessions, a beautifully made circular wooden bowl about six inches in diameter. There is a delicate inlaid pattern around the bowl and the lid fits perfectly.

It was made by 'Wilsa', 'King of the School', a leader; a rebel; always avid for excitement and new experience; antagonistic to authority and discipline. He could cause trouble and get into trouble with equal ease. He was admired by most for his toughness and feared by some for his ruthless pursuit of what he considered justice. Yet he had a great concealed gentleness and understanding, and his own integral sense of right and wrong. He always showed loyalty, respect and affection so far as I personally was concerned.

He made the box as part of his practical work for the CSE Examination and gained a first class pass.

On the last day of my teaching life his sister came to the Staff Room and handed me a brown paper bag, saying, 'Our David sent you this.'

It was the bowl. I think of him each time I look at it and am glad that he is now a happily married family man.

I could indulge myself with many such affectionate memories as I look around my home, and at the book of newspaper clippings I have kept about events in the life of the school over quarter of a century. Instead, I'll begin at the beginning.

9.

New Delaval Secondary Modern School was originally a 'pit school', built by the local colliery owners about 1860 for the education of the miners' children. The workmen paid a fee of a penny a week for each Infant and twopence a week for each older child. These fees were still in force even after the 1870 Education Act made child-education compulsory.

In times of especial hardship school attendance was low as parents could not always afford 'school money'. This is particularly apparent from entries made in the school log book in 1887, when a miners' strike lasted from January until nearly the end of May

11th Feb. 1887. The miners are still out on strike. The attendance has been poor. Many children paid no school money.

25th Feb. 1887. A large number of children have been unable to pay their fees on account of the strike.

27th May, 1887. The miners have commenced work today and consequently it is to be hoped that the average attendance will improve.

In 1891 the Board of Education recommended that school fees be abolished or much reduced; the Delaval log book records

4th Sept. 1891. It has been decided by the Managers to free the Infant School entirely and to make a charge of a penny a week in each of the Standards in the Mixed School, the children having their books and other materials supplied to them free of charge.

The school was originally an integral part of the long rows of terraced houses with long narrow front gardens, small backyards and back street privies which made up a mining village.

By the time I knew the school the mine had been closed and the houses pulled down, so it stood almost alone. In the distant background were the pit heaps, where spoil had for so many years been tipped, and the derelict pit. The manager's house, though empty and dilapidated, was still standing, but what had once been streets of houses and gardens was now wasteland where vestiges of gardens still survived. The children knew where to find rhubarb, raspberries, gooseberries and mint in season. Sometimes they brought flowers, hardy perennials, found growing in some hidden spot.

There were two pit ponds up the wasteland with frogs, minnows, newts, drowned cats and dogs and old prams and bedsteads. There were many birds nests and, at the old mine shaft, owls. There were always larks shrilling in the air; indeed local place names such as Laverick Hall Road and Laverick Hall Farm bore witness to the prolificy of this bird. (Laverick is an old name for lark.)

A path, which had once been a wagon way from Plessey Pit to Blyth Harbour, came past the school and we could walk up the path through fields to where there had once been a blacksmith's shop beside the main road. This was known as 'going up the Laverick'.

The colliery village had two Methodist chapels. One, now isolated 'up the Laverick' was used as a storage place by the local Co-op, the other still in use, was in the school grounds.

The school comprised a number of buildings enclosed on the south and west by a brick wall, by a wooden fence on the north and by New Delaval Miners' Park and Welfare Hall on the east.

I entered that first morning by the gate in the southern wall, which opened into the boys' playground, a small area. Jutting into it was the main building, the corner room of which was the Headmaster's office, a small square room with its door opening into the boys' playground.

A narrow flagged passage separated the school building from the back wall of the caretaker's house which, in the old 'pit-school' days, had been the Headmaster's residence. Stretching away in front of this house was a garden, long and wide, with lawns, fruit trees, flowers and vegetable patches. It had become the school garden, maintained entirely by the gardening classes. The tool shed in the far corner had once been used to stable the Headmaster's horse.

In 1936, against the wall, midway down the garden three wooden classrooms had been erected, equipped for Domestic Science, General Science and Woodwork.

The Staff lavatory was in the corner of the garden nearest the house.

The room on the left of the caretaker's front door was used as a Staff Room.

If you walked along the narrow passage way between the end of the main school building and the back of the caretaker's house you emerged into a big playground, the Girls' yard, with the chapel opening out of it. Congregations, funeral corteges and wedding parties had to cross the length of the Girls' yard to enter the chapel.

The Infant School was a separate brick building at the far side of the yard, separated from the rest of the school complex by a wooden fence.

I threaded my way, that first Monday, through swarms of running, shouting boys, knocked on the green painted door on the corner of the building and entered the Headmaster's office.

He was sitting at his desk, looking towards the door, a little elderly man with yellowy transparent skin and pale expressionless eyes. He gazed at me without speaking. I said, 'Good-morning, Mr Maxey. My name is Wrigley, I think you are expecting me. I've been sent here as a supply teacher.

He said, 'I don't know why they sent *you* here. We were doing very well with Mrs Coulson.'

To which I replied, 'Well, I didn't want to come. I was quite happy where I was.'

Such was my welcome to Delaval.

Mr. Maxey had in earlier years been a good teacher and, later, an efficient Headmaster, but he was now in poor health, prematurely aged, and listless. Changes were irritating.

I was the latest in a succession of supply teachers who had replaced the Geography teacher when he returned to the Army in which he had served during the First World War. All but one of the male teachers were now in the Armed Services and the school was suffering in consequence.

Mr. Maxey told me I would teach Geography to all the classes, English Literature to Form IIIA of which I would be Form Mistress, Arithmetic once a week to a class of slow-learners for which he was himself responsible and Physical Education to a year group of boys. I should find a timetable on the classroom wall, a syllabus and record book in the teacher's desk.

Then he walked slowly to the door and bade me follow him.

By this time a bell had been rung somewhere in the building and the children had entered the school and gone to their classrooms for registration.

We entered the school by a door opposite the caretaker's back door into a small lobby area, through another door into a long corridor with a short one crossing it at right angles, so that the corridors made a crucifix shape, with one classroom opening off each side of the top of the cross and two opening off each side of the longer section. At the end of each arm of the short corridor were the cloakrooms with washbasins and pegs, girls' at one end, boys' at the other. The lavatories were outside in the yards.

I was led into the single classroom on the right where more than thirty turbulent teenagers were assembled, a few sitting talking, the rest jostling around or mock-wrestling.

They quietened somewhat as the Headmaster entered. He yelled to them to sit down and be quiet, showed me where the syllabus, record book and register were, introduced me briefly and went away.

Once more, I felt very small and the children overwhelming, but they were reasonably quiet, obviously weighing me up.

The first period with any new class, especially in a school to which one is a stranger, is most important. The pupils are sizing you up, weighing the possibilities; you have to assess them without seeming to do so, and try to establish contact without being either bossy or ingratiating. The best thing to do is to arouse their interest and plunge them and yourself into work, so that incipient rebels don't have time to plan disruption. I left registration till later.

I felt no great confidence in myself as a Geography teacher and decided to leave a formal approach to the subject until I could study the syllabus carefully and made adequate preparations.

I began with a story.

All youngsters like stories and even thirteen-year-olds are not too sophisticated to enjoy Kipling's *Rikki Tikki Tavi*, a simple but exciting story of a mongoose which saved the life of a little boy being attacked by a cobra. I had come prepared, a copy of the *Jungle Book* in my bag, I sat down, opened the book, said, 'Listen to this,' and began to read.

The restlessness and curiosity subsided; the class became absorbed in the detail of the story.

When it ended, I began to talk about India and ask if they could tell me anything about it. Some had brothers or uncles there, in the Army or the RAF around Bombay or Calcutta. I said there must be a map of India somewhere in the room.

A swoop to show me where maps were kept seemed imminent, so I asked a girl near the cupboard to find the map. Then I chose a tall boy who I felt would be better to have as an ally than an opponent and said, 'You're much taller than I am, so will you lower the blackboard on the easel for me, please, and we'll hang the map up.'

He complied with a sort of swaggering embarrassment and smiled when I thanked him.

Shortly afterwards the school bell rang, announcing morning break. I marked the register as they drank their milk. They went out, eyeing me speculatively as they passed my desk and I smiled at them, each one an individual I hoped soon to understand.

10.

There were sets of quite good Geography text books and atlases, and I planned lessons ahead at home, bolstering text book facts with excerpts from travel books and biographies to try to give places a reality in the imagination which they had never had for me in my school days. One boy I met later as a man, said that at the time he really thought I had been to the Himalayas and seen an Everest expedition in preparation.

I gathered as many relevant pictures and photographs as possible. I tried to make the young ones realize that the River Blyth on the map was the one they crossed by stepping-stones at Humford Woods, and fished as it made its way between the piers into the sea at Blyth. I wished we could have had an amenity which is now commonplace – a school bus, so that the Geography of the county could be learned in a practical way.

But there was a need to draw maps, find facts individually, and make notes and the pupils had no notebooks. It was before the day of the biro, so there were pens with horrible nibs which were easy to cross-point, ink wells into which blotting paper and pieces of chewing-gum could be pushed, forty pencils which I had to keep sharpened, and a number of india-rubbers for erasing, but no paper. I approached Mr Maxey.

He said, 'What do you want to bother with drawing maps and writing notes for? Just let them read books.' I said map-making and individual notes were essential.

Reluctantly, he gave me six notebooks and told me to tear them up into separate sheets of paper.

I had only been back in the classroom a few minutes when a boy came in and said, 'Mr Maxey says he gave you too many writing books. I have to take three back.'

Eventually, I bought packets of loose leaf myself so that we could make meagre folders of maps and notes.

Mr Maxey seemed to have a phobia about wasting paper; perhaps in his mind it was part of his war effort because people were always being exhorted not to waste any.

He taught Arithmetic four times a week to the class I taught once, and the exercise books looked appalling. Each page was divided into three columns and sums were cramped close in each, with no spacing. Added to this, corrections had to be crammed in beside any sum marked incorrect. The pages were smudgy and incomprehensive. Moreover, the whole class did exactly the same mechanical exercises, working from printed books of set sums, with none of the individual attention needed by slow-learners.

I could do nothing about the spacing of the sums except try to encourage neatness, but I did try to awaken interest.

Personally, I like to be given a reason for anything I am asked or expected to do and believe children should have work made acceptable in the same way.

There was one boy with an innate brightness, but little concentration. He did not like arithmetic but he loved rabbits; he could wrinkle his nose just like one. So in a manner of speaking, I mated rabbits to Arithmetic for him.

We bought definite numbers of rabbits at specific prices; we sold some and gave some away, then reckoned how many were left; we decided what quantity of food would be required per day, worked out the quantity needed for a week and how much money would be required to pay for it; we calculated how much money we would need to save each week to buy a camera to take photographs when the baby rabbits were born in a few weeks time.

Then I suggested measuring the dimensions of a hutch and working out how much timber we should need to purchase to make one. At this point, he said, 'Oh, have a heart, miss. You're putting me off rabbits.'

I saw his point and tried to find a new slant. I hope he still likes rabbits.

The classes were large, the behaviour at times, boisterous and unruly, and much of my Geography teaching dull. At the beginning of each lesson it was necessary to gain control and establish a good atmosphere in which to work. If pupils came from a room where they had been out of control for a lengthy period, establishing contact and order took longer. I persevered, using will power, keeping my temper under control, trying never to raise my voice, and insisting on a standard of individual effort.

If time was wasted in class, I expected the idlers to make up for it after the rest went home. They called this 'being kept-in'. These detention periods were fruitful not so much for the work completed as for the opportunity it gave me to get to know the culprits better. Having finished their work, they would gather round me as I checked it and chatter about their friends, homes, pets and pastimes and ask me questions about myself, quite different people from the rebellious show-offs of early afternoon.

Sometimes, if permitted, friends stayed to wait for them. One night, a boy who did excellent individual work and spent much of his own time on it, waited in this way, leaning against my desk, chatting quietly. After a while, I said, 'Robert, you could be getting on with your project while you're waiting.'

He considered a moment, then replied, 'No, that would be being kept-in, wouldn't it? I'm coming early tomorrow morning to do it before the school bell rings.'

The better we got to know one another, the easier discipline became. I was able to show appreciation of their humour, they accepted mine.

I had to do a Physical Education session for an hour once a week with a year-group of boys. There used to be an obligatory official printed syllabus of PE lessons or tables for use in all schools. A teacher was supposed to memorise the table for the specific day and carry out the progressions, which began with the class standing in four files graded according to height. There were head and neck exercises, interspersed by 'breaks' when the files broke loose and practised activities on the move. The lesson concluded with a game.

I hated the 'breaks' which could become chaotic, boys running in all directions, narrowly missing me, and not 'able to hear' the whistle being frantically blown to recall them to their files.

One day I went into the little walled-in yard where we performed these manoeuvres to find the lads in their files, but with the tallest ones (a head above me) at the front and the smallest ones at the back. Portraying neither indignation nor surprise, I walked to the other end of the files, and ordered, 'With a jump, about turn!'

They automatically obeyed and began to laugh, and so did I. It gave me a useful step-up in their estimation.

Eventually I broke the official rule and ignored the tables, concentrating instead on team agilities or games with balls, which they more or less organized themselves.

The way in which English was divided as a subject I found most unsatisfactory, one teacher doing Grammar and Exercises, another Composition, a third Literature. To me Language and Literature are integral: you can't have one without the other. I like to savour words and phrases and develop creative writing from reading. Instead, I had one isolated lesson each week, reading a set book with IIIA.

But it was a cosy lesson. Thirty odd years on I still meet a man or woman in a street or shop, an apparent stranger, who will stop and greet me saying, 'Do you remember me? Delaval School?' Then acquaintance renewed I'll be asked, 'Do you remember when we read – ?' Then will come a title; *Prester John, Poo Lorn, Shane, Rikki-tikki, Lord of the Flies,* etc.

Mr Maxey's health continued to decline. He would frequently fall asleep in the chair in his office. At other times, he would wander slowly and listlessly around the school and into classrooms, without any apparent purpose.

He used to try different health fads and one I vividly remember – dried prunes. He used to carry them in an outer pocket of his jacket, put one in his mouth as he wandered into the classroom, chew it slowly then spit the stone in the direction of the wastepaper basket. The procedure would mesmerise all of us; it was impossible not to be interested in the accuracy of the ejection.

His mind would follow a train of thought and he would suddenly make a remark or ask a question relating to what he had silently been thinking, usually something quite irrelevant to the work in progress.

One day when there had been a German air attack over north-west England, a school was hit and a teacher killed. Details of this were given on the radio and in newspapers.

The following morning Mr Maxey came into IIIA classroom, eyed the assembled pupils in silence for a few minutes, then demanded, 'What would you do?.

There was of course, no reply.

'Come on! What would you do?'

Eventually, we guessed the incident to which he was referring and one girl said, 'I would scream, sir.'

'Yes' he said, 'YOU would.'

Then he pointed to someone else and said 'What would you do?'

'Wait until Mrs Wrigley told us what to do,' was the reply.

'A lot of use that would be,' retorted Mr Maxey, 'Mrs Wrigley's dead.'

In November 1943, a letter from the Director of Education informed me that I must report the following Friday, 1st December, to Princess Louise Road Senior Girls' School, the place where I had so happily taught prior to my marriage. My old job was vacant and the Headmistress had requested my return.

I should have been overjoyed; instead, I felt a sadness.

Mr Maxey said, 'I don't know why they want to move you. You're managing all right here.'

IIIA Literature was last lesson Thursday and at that time, we were reading *Prester John*. When four o'clock came on that particular Thursday, Dave was still shut up in the huge mountain cavern with the treasure and the great dying John Laputa.

I said, 'I'm leaving tonight, so if any of you wish to stay a little longer, I'll finish the story.'

They all stayed and afterwards waved to me as I rode away on my bicycle.

Back at Princess Louise Road Girls' School I was welcomed by Staff and girls.

Discipline was natural and friendly. I taught English all day, following my own syllabus, with plenty of books and writing material, to industrious friendly girls.

The atmosphere was congenial, conditions as perfect as they could be, but my life seemed to be short of something.

I lived not far from Croft Park, Blyth Spartans' Football field and most Delaval boys were Spartans supporters. One Saturday afternoon shortly after I had left Delaval, the door bell rang and there stood a group of boys.

They had called to see me before the football match and brought me two pictures, red tulips with green leaves, cut out of 'silver' paper, mounted on black paper, and framed. I was truly touched.

Christmas-time came and with it a card signed by everyone in Form IIIA at Delaval School. Inscribed on the back was, 'We all wish you were back at Delaval School.' I realized then that I wished that too.

The opportunity to do so came in August, 1944, Mr Maxey was forced to retire because of extreme ill health, leaving the school in a very run-down condition, all masters except one away in the Armed Forces.

Mr Sydney Soulsby, previously a master at Princess Louise Road Boys' School was selected as the new Headmaster for Delaval and he requested that I should be appointed to the Staff.

Again a note from the Education Committee directing me to leave Princess Louise Road Girls' School at the end of the summer term and to present myself at Delaval Secondary Modern School on the first day of the autumn term.

Miss Wilson was reluctant to release me and requested the Education Committee to reconsider their decision, but I inwardly hoped the directive would stand, and it did.

So again I bade farewell to the Staff and girls at Princess Louise Road School and left, laden with presents and flowers, saddened by tears, and feeling that this time I should not be returning.

I had decided that as long as I continued to teach I would stay at Delaval School provided they wanted me.

11.

I recall happily the August morning in 1944 when I returned to Delaval School, (retitled, because of the new Education Act, Delaval Secondary Modern School), where I became officially Deputy Head in 1949 and retained this post until I retired in 1970.

On the way that first morning I met Mr Soulsby, the new Headmaster, who had been a colleague at Princess Louise Road Boys' School. He greeted me warmly and began at once to outline his plans for building up a good school and I shared his enthusiasm.

The old building was the same except that it was more dilapidated. The yards were now smaller as they contained long ugly red brick air-raid shelters. The store-room (originally a small classroom) just inside the school entrance, was now used exclusively by the ARP, a group of air-raid wardens, as an official communications post. It was manned day and night and a telephone had been installed. When the war ended and the post was dismantled Mr Soulsby asked if the school could retain the telephone, but his request was refused.

Until school 'phones became regarded as essential some years later, any necessary calls had to be made from a public call-box about a hundred yards down the road.

The paint work in the school was scratched and faded, the desks shabby and defaced, the rooms bare and the pupils unused to order, effort or discipline. It was a privilege to help in its restoration and a joy to see it change from a forlorn community of reluctant and sometimes rebellious pupils to an entity of enthusiastic, friendly, loyal and predominantly self-disciplined individuals.

The school had no hall and I don't think the children had ever been gathered en masse. Boys and girls had lined up in their respective yards and gone straight to their appointed classrooms.

Mr Soulsby decided at once that there must be a morning assembly where he could speak to everyone, establish contact and give some idea of his aims and intentions. So each morning, from the very beginning, the pupils lined up, class by class, in three arms of the cross formed by the corridors and the Headmaster stood at a table in the fourth section, where there was also a piano. Members of staff stood with their classes, with the exception of the music teacher, who sat at the piano.

I always kept a vase of flowers on the table, either wild ones gathered in local woods and hedgerows, culled from the school garden, or brought by pupils.

Later, when my husband returned from the RAF in 1946, to his post as Woodwork and Gardening master, one of the boys made a little polished oak cross on a plinth and thenceforward this stood on the table for morning assembly too.

Mr Soulsby was himself a Nonconformist with a genuine simple faith and a strong resonant voice. From the earliest days he conducted a simple service with a reading, a prayer and some robust hymn-singing. When the male complement of the staff was restored there were one or two with good voices, so we soon had harmonising, descants and plenty of good swelling sound.

Many hymns were favourites of Mr Soulsby – 'Guide me, oh thou great Jehovah', 'Rock of Ages', 'Onward Christian Soldiers', 'The King of Love my Shepherd is' – but there were also simple ones such as 'Morning has broken like the first morning', and 'Lord of all Hopefulness, Lord of all joy'.

One year it was decided to enter a school group in the hymn-singing contest at the County Music Festival. As the music teacher wished to play the piano accompaniment herself, Mr Soulsby decided to be the conductor. He had no previous experience or special skill, but infinite enthusiasm and endeavour.

They practised 'Praise my soul, the King of Heaven' with great diligence and returned triumphantly from the festival with third prize.

One memory of hymn-singing in assembly I shall always keep is of the goalkeeper of the school football team, a stalwart lad just under six feet tall, who in later years played for Blyth Spartans, singing with sincere fervour 'God make my life a little flower'.

In autumn, we used to have a harvest service with produce from home and school gardens piled on the table. Then 'we ploughed the fields and scattered', and 'when all was safely gathered in', arranged for the produce to be taken to elderly or needy people in the locality.

But all this came long after that first morning when the faces of the assembled pupils portrayed mostly curiosity, sullenness or disinterest.

They would see their new Headmaster as a man of medium build with greying hair and a pale complexion. He was not physically strong as he was still affected by injuries sustained in the First World War. He had been an ambulance-bearer at the Battle of the Somme. But he had a strong sonorous voice, a ready smile, and a sympathetic understanding of young people.

He outlined his plans, explained what he expected of them and what he hoped to provide for them. He said that to have a good happy school there must be friendliness, discipline, pride and effort. His sincerity and enthusiasm evoked some small signs of interest before we went to our respective classrooms and the uphill task began.

Each teacher was responsible for one particular form and spent the first half-hour of each day with it, after which the pupils moved from room to room according to their timetable.

My form was IIIA, the most senior in the school and there were usually about thirty members. I explained straightaway that the classroom was our living-room, just like a room at home, so we should keep it tidy, comfy and welcoming, with pictures on the walls, flowers on the window ledges and litter only in the waste-paper basket.

I took vases bought at jumble sales or charity stalls, old ginger jars etc., and soon children were adding to the collection. We kept them in a cupboard and chose suitable ones for the flowers available. Monday morning 9.15 to 9.30 was 'flower morning' and girls kept the vases topped-up as needed during the week. All the year round, I gathered flowers, leaves and berries at the weekend and arranged them in a big bowl on a bookcase beside my desk. It was never empty, from twigs and catkins in January to holly, ivy and fir branches in December, with the gamut of the year's colour and variety in between.

I had brought the bookcase from home and kept in it a varied selection of books and magazines which could be freely picked up for casual reading.

Other flowers were brought from home gardens or picked by pupils on the sandhills or 'up the Laverick' and were arranged in little pots and vases on the window ledges.

They often brought me button holes too, complete with pin, and in summer I was never without at least one rose pinned to my lapel, with others waiting in water to take their place later in the day. In early May they brought lily-of-the-valley, the fragrance of which now gives me nostalgic recall.

Over the years, Mr Soulsby built up a collection of framed pictures to share among the classrooms, and posters and cut-out pictures relating to lessons were pinned up as required, but one thing was always fixed on a wall of whichever classroom I was responsible for from that first week until I finished teaching in 1970, when I left it on the classroom wall.

At first, it was inscribed by me in mediocre script, on drawing-paper. Then a boy came from the art room one day with it beautifully printed and bound round the edges with coloured tape. Later, another boy voluntarily made a frame for it and put it under glass. It read:-

> If you would have kindness, be kind,
> If you would have truth, be true;
> What you give of yourself, you find;
> The world's a reflection of you.

Not good poetically maybe, but it instills the right idea. Cleverness does not matter as much as kindness, and everyone can be kind.

Quite often girls or boys would ask me to write this in their autograph books, and there it would be, inscribed among the 'Roses are red, violets are blue' and 'By hook or by crook I'll be last in this book.'

12.

We spent August settling in; becoming acquainted with the pupils, establishing a work-order; stock-taking.

Most of the gardening and woodwork tools had been lost, broken or stolen, and had to be replaced ready for when a teacher became available, but we found scores of packets of thick empty exercise books with paper of first-class quality. I smiled ruefully thinking of how Mr Maxey had been hoarding this store when he only allowed me three books and I had to buy loose-leaf myself.

Although our aim was to provide an education of breadth, variety and individuality, built on a sound base of literacy (the 'three Rs') we felt we must first try to establish a communal feeling in the school and awaken ideals.

So, in September, Mr Soulsby invited an 'Old Boy' of Delaval School to come and talk to the assembled pupils and he gained permission to use the adjoining Miners' Welfare Hall for the occasion. The 'Old Boy' was Captain Whitfield Foy, BA, BD, Chaplain to the 6th Airborne Division. He gave a vivid account of the D Day landings and enthralled his young audience; they were obviously proud to know he had, as a boy, attended their school.

In October, Mr Soulsby took some of the seniors on a tour of the local gasworks and everyone visited the submarine base in Blyth Harbour. Some seniors accompanied me to the Theatre Royal at Newcastle to see *Merchant of Venice*.

By such means, we were establishing personal contact and widening the perspective of our youngsters.

There was, at first, only one man on the Staff, elderly, of some erudition with strong political ideals but no understanding of children. Even during brief coffee breaks in the staffroom he bored the rest of us with his eulogies of Karl Marx and Beatrice and Sydney Webb. He tried, without success, to teach

History and was always irate in the classroom. He punished unnecessarily and ineffectually: the boys deliberately aggravated him; the girls remained sullen.

The boys were more deprived than the girls. There was no man to teach Woodwork or Gardening, nor to supervise Physical Education and Games. The girls had the benefit of good stable teaching in Needlework and Domestic Science.

With the majority of male teachers away in the Armed Forces considerable reliance had to be placed on women supply teachers who sometimes only stayed for short periods.

At a Staff meeting Mr Soulsby outlined his plans for improving the standard of academic attainment in the school.

His aims were that:-

1. every pupil should be given encouragement to reach a personal goal;
2. a firm, albeit friendly, discipline should be enforced in the classroom so that the atmosphere would be congenial to concentrated work;
3. each pupil should realize that he or she could present written work which looked tidy and legible. Neat careful work was to be commended, slovenly careless work rejected.

He emphasised that enthusiasm and interest would produce better results than a forced discipline.

Alongside academic attainment, he wanted to establish pride in the school and awareness of good qualities. To this end, he decided to introduce the House System: each pupil would be allocated to one specific House when he or she first entered the school and would maintain allegiance to it thereafter.

Brothers and sisters were given membership of the same House. Before my teaching career ended I knew eleven-year-olds who asked to be made members of the House to which their mother or father (in one instance both) had belonged, and this was usually arranged.

House points (a red ink star) could be gained by academic achievement, well presented work; outstanding personal effort etc. Points could be deducted (a black ink square) for lack of effort; carelessness; anti-social behaviour etc. Each form teacher made a simple chart to pin up on the classroom wall.

Once a year all the stars were added, the black marks deducted, a House average calculated and an award made to the winning House.

Mr Soulsby's choice of House names was inspired: Stephenson; Grace Darling; Montgomery; Buchanan.

George Stephenson was born at Wylam where his birthplace can still be seen on the banks of the River Tyne. His father was a colliery fireman and George became assistant to his father when he was fourteen. Of his own accord, he went to night school to learn to read and write. Later he worked an engine at Killingworth Colliery and dismantled it once a week until he thoroughly understood its construction. He built his first locomotive in 1814, supervised the laying of a railway line between Stockton and Darlington in 1829 and built *The Rocket* steam engine.

His mining background was similar to that of the majority of our pupils, he was a local boy and a fine example of sustained personal endeavour.

Grace Darling was born at Bamburgh, a few miles up the coast, daughter of a lighthouse keeper on the Farne Islands. When she was eighteen years old she rowed out with her father in a storm to rescue nine seamen clinging to a rock, survivors of the wrecked ship, *Forfar*. She received a gold medal for her courage. The boat in which they went to the rescue and other mementoes are in the tiny Grace Darling museum at Bamburgh. Her tomb is in the churchyard.

Her youth, the fact that she also was local, her courage and self-sacrifice appealed to our youngsters and set them an example.

General Montgomery, of Desert Army fame, was an example of courage and leadership. Mr Soulsby actually wrote to General Montgomery, who was still engaged in the Second World War, and asked his approval. He received a personal reply in which General Montgomery expressed his pleasure in having a House named after him. This letter was duly framed and given a place of honour in the school.

John Buchanan was one of a large family born in a Glasgow slum and neglected from birth. He was physically handicapped, entirely without fingers and with only a little stump of a thumb. He was sent to the National Children's Home at Chipping Norton. There he soon became outstanding for his tenacity and perseverance, insisting on doing, despite his disability, whatever any able-bodied child tried to do. For instance, he tied unaided the knots required of a Boy Scout.

It was discovered that he could draw well using his fingerless palms and eventually he reached Oxford School of Art, where he was an outstanding student. He did exquisite illuminated lettering and was soon working full-time and making a good income doing illustrations, designing greeting cards and calendars and illuminating personal cards for people. His patrons included members of the Royal Family.

Instead of enjoying personal affluence and luxury, Buchanan chose to live in a small house near the National Children's Homes, one of whose nurses he eventually married. He retained an adequate income for himself and devoted the rest of his earnings and time to helping the Homes.

Mr Soulsby wrote to Buchanan who replied in an exquisitely written letter expressing the pleasure and honour he felt in having a House named after him. He asked if he could have details to enable him to make a coat-of-arms for the school.

Our motto, 'Never Despair' had already been chosen.

In due course we received the coat of arms and had it suitably framed.

It was quartered, with Stephenson's Rocket in one section, crossed oars over a zigzag of lightning in another for Grace Darling, the Eighth Army flash for Montgomery and a palette with paint brushes representing Buchanan. At the top was inscribed NEW DELAVAL SENIOR SCHOOL, at the bottom NEVER DESPAIR. It became a source of pride to every boy, girl and teacher who passed through the school.

Recently, the Delaval Secondary Modern School became a Middle School, with pupils aged 9–13 from a wide area, a different Staff and Headmaster and no tradition. A former colleague of mine, a member of the Staff, found the coat-of-arms removed and about to be thrown away so that the frame could be used for another purpose. He rescued it and brought it to me and it hangs on a wall here in my home, another treasured memento.

Each House was given a colour, and teachers were appointed to each house. It was with pride that I became a Staff member of Buchanan House (green) and my husband joined me when he returned from the RAF.

Next, Mr Soulsby approached the owners of the school premises, Hartley Main Collieries Ltd., and suggested that they might like to provide a silver cup to be used for inter-House competition. They subsequently provided a handsome silver cup with a wooden plinth on which were mounted silver shields ready for inscriptions.

Named the Hartley Main Cup, it was formally presented at a ceremony in the Miners' Welfare Hall, presided over by Alderman Aaron Walton, Mayor of Blyth. It was handed over by Colonel Lumsden, DSO and received on behalf of the Local Education Authority by a school governor, Alderman Reilly.

This was on December 19th, 1944, four months after my return to Delaval, and it was on Christmas Eve, a few days later, that the boys and girls of my Form came carol-singing at the door and gave me my cherished wooden candlesticks.

Later, the school acquired another trophy. Mr Soulsby gave the silver Soulsby Sports Cup which was awarded annually to the House which had gained most points on average in inter-House competition, taking in netball, football, rounders, cricket and athletics.

A major award was inaugurated in 1947. This was an individual honour which did not require academic ability or athletic skill. It was known as the Scott Fellowship, after Scott of the Antarctic, and could only be won by someone whose behaviour and attitude enhanced the prestige of the school and set an example of courage and cheerful perseverance. It was not easily gained and much coveted.

The actual award was always a copy of *The Great White South*. When the award was inaugurated Peter Scott, later Sir Peter, son of the explorer and himself a renowned artist and ornithologist, visited the school.

We all gathered in the cross of the corridors. He talked to us about his father's courage and endurance and how it was his father's wish that he should lead an outdoor life – hence his interest in wild life. He showed us the rings he used to mark migrant birds and described his work at Slimbridge. He autographed the Scott Fellowship books, listened to the pupils singing north-country folk songs, and then had tea in the Domestic Science Room with the members of the Fellowship, the Headmaster and the Staff.

In later years, when he came to lecture in the area, successive Fellowship members were able to take their Scott books to be autographed.

Everyone in the school could wear two badges, and most did; a button badge in the House colour and a specially made metal school badge. It had a lark in the centre (the Laverick we heard trilling each spring and summer day) and on the outer edge of the circle, Never Despair. New Delaval Senior School.

13.

The Second World War was still in progress and everyone was encouraged to purchase National Savings certificates. There was rivalry between schools to contribute most in any one week and results were published in the local weekly *Blyth News*.

We seemed to do well, regular quantities of National Savings stamps being purchased each Monday morning from the teacher in charge of the scheme. Later we discovered that a considerable number of buyers were cashing certificates at the Post Office the following week to obtain cash with which to buy more Savings stamps at the school. So much for statistics.

We had a grand effort for the Wings for Victory Week Fund. Monday afternoon, from 2.30 to 4.00 pm was given over to the project and each class arranged its own money-making scheme. There were sales of cakes and home-made sweets, raffles, hoop-la and throwing balls into buckets in the schoolyard and other competitions requiring luck or physical skill. Form IIIA had a rabbit-show.

Before the lunch-break the boys placed all the desks singly around three sides of the room with the lids lifted and fastened back. All the books they had contained were stacked away in cupboards by the girls. Two boys brought straw from a local farm and we lined the desks with it.

In the afternoon, those who owned pet rabbits brought them and we put one in each desk with a label stating its name, age, type etc.

Not much attention was paid to the Literature lesson which was on the timetable for the first part of the afternoon as all eyes and minds were on the rabbits. They were remarkably docile and well-behaved with the exception of one which was restless and anxious to climb into any desk except its own. It reminded me very much of its owner.

At half past two, Mr Cowell, secretary of a local rabbit club came and did the judging and prize cards were fastened to the desks of the winning rabbits.

Then the rest of the school were able to visit the show and give their own unique critical appraisal. As each was charged sixpence (2½p) for admission, we had a highly successful afternoon.

At 4.30 pm we were still ushering out spectators reluctant to leave, but the rabbits had to be returned to ventilated boxes or tucked inside owners' jackets, the straw removed and burnt and the desks washed clean and put back in place ready for normal use the following morning.

In that week's edition of *Blyth News* the following report appeared:-

---

NEW DELAVAL SHOW OF RABBITS.

A rabbit show, organised by children of the top class was held at New Delaval School on Monday, proceeds for Wings for Victory Week Fund. Mr. Cowell was Judge.
Prize winners:-   1. Stanley Palmer (Marten Sable)
                     2. Edith Chapman (Flemish Giant)
                     3. Tom Straker (English Butterfly)

The boys had no formal Physical Education, but someone was usually available to supervise football and cricket sessions on a local playing-field known as Gallahers. Sometimes I took groups of boys and girls together for walks 'up the Laverick'; it would be truer to say they took me. And this practice continued over the years on occasions when there was a shortage of Staff and I took two classes together.

They led me on explorations and bird-watching expeditions 'up the Laverick' and 'on the heaps' (from whence we could see the Cheviot Hills in the distance), so that my intimate knowledge of the locality expanded, also my understanding of the psychology of youth, and friendships which I still enjoy were established over the years.

I have a rough plan, drawn by a boy, outlining the area and bearing the names they gave to specific places, names which were familiar to successive generations of children until the heaps were levelled to become a golf course and the Goblin became a hazard, lost golf balls replacing the dead cats, old beds and bicycles of yore.

The Yellow Babby was a rusty stream which flowed from the disused pit, with bullrushes and one old hawthorn tree. The youngsters fought by it, fell in it, bridged it and dammed it, engineered waterfalls and stepping-stones and made stories and poems about it. Along it, one could find toads, shrews, rats, hardy wild flowers, nests of larks and reed-buntings and a so-called 'rabbits' drinking place'.

Nesting near the old pit were larks, meadow-pipits, whitethroats, yellow-hammers, buntings, greenfinches, linnets and wheatears.

One boy in particular, 'Mally' knew the habitat of all these birds and won an inter-school public speaking contest talking about them. Now mature, Malcolm Thompson is an active member of the Northumberland Wildlife Trust and I sometimes meet him in the woods, binoculars slung around his neck, accompanied by his two small sons. Once, when he was a boy he took my husband and me up the River Blyth to see dippers, disclosing the haunts of other birds on the way.

Delaval children, from an early age, spent evenings, weekends and holidays on or near 'the heaps'; it was a world of its own, a place of adventure and fantasy.

One pond they named 'the Goblin'. Here are some accounts of life 'on the heaps' written in English lessons.

"We reach the Goblin by a small valley from the road. It is marshy near the edge and has one steep bank made of pit heap, the rest is grass. Once we built a bridge across with old timber from the pit. We float a log in as a target and aim stones at it or take airguns and shoot at a floating tin. It is about $2^1/2$ ft. deep in the middle, and in winter, if it freezes, we skate on it."

"There is salt at the edge when water evaporates, we tasted it and it was salty. Wagtails went round the edge pecking. Once we found a dead fox in the water in a bag, slashed as if it had been caught in a snare. We thought it was a dog until we found its tail, it made the water putrid for a time. We stotted bricks off it to try to sink it. Then we put it on an old door and tried to sail it. At last it rotted away."

"We made a raft of pit props, two layers fastened with string, and more piled on top. Once we made one from an old window frame from Myers. We attached another raft in the middle, playing torpedoes. Sometimes we fell in."

"There is a little pond further away, along a grassy path with a hawthorn tree in the middle of the path. There are water rats with shiny coats among the reeds and we catch sticklebacks."

"Red Rock Canyon is near the pit. It looks molten with red rock from the pit. There are steep stark cliffs all round. At the top, in the centre, is a pile of rocks with two large flat ones on top. We sit there to fire catapults. It is a bad place to be caught by Cowpeners. It is an advantage for throwing stones but you can easily be surrounded."

"At Red Rock Canyon we play war games, like Japs and English. We put old hinges or bits of metal into the cliff, or sleeper bolts, and climb up by them.
We play duffs, jumping from steep heights into the dust below, up to the knees sometimes. It is hard to keep your balance and get your feet in first."

"We dug a cave in Red Rock Canyon. At first, we were just looking for fossils but it grew to a cave. We put props in to support it and make it realistic. It was about four feet high and two feet in. It was tough rock and hard to cart out. Then at the pit we found some old picks, and a round coal shovel without a handle in the Goblin and we brought hammers from home. We used to sit in and eat."

"Gamblers' Den is a hollow in the heaps where gamblers from Cowpen, Newsham and Blyth play pitch and toss on Sunday afternoons. They throw two halfcrowns up, they always play with halfcrowns. Once we lay on top of the steep slope and tried to catch halfcrowns with a net on a stick. We used to throw snowballs at them in winter and they used to chase us. When it was cold they lit a fire to play beside. Sometimes there were arguments and fights."

"Once there was a scatter in Gamblers' Den when a police motor-bike came along the field path. Sometimes we threw bangers in, two or three tied together. A tramp stayed there once, slept on an old mattress. We chased him and threw bangers. He was a little dark-skinned man with a beard. He wore an old RAF greatcoat. Later he shifted to a railway hut along the line."

Two other named spots were Myers and Hackers.
Myers was the remains of what had been the colliery manager's house and garden, now reduced to rubble, matted weeds, bushes, trees and a few hardy perennials. This was mostly frequented by girls who picked flowers, gossiped in the sunshine, and played games of fantasy and imagination.

Hackers was a place of activity most weekdays, when unemployed men used to rummage for coal among the slag dumped by engine-drawn wagons from an adjacent colliery. They hacked it out, put it into sacks and wheeled them away on rusty old bicycles. Some of them were aggressive if disturbed.

But in September 1945 when I was first taken 'up the Laverick' its geography was new to me. The youngsters identified birds, rummaged derelict gardens, found frogs, shrews and mice, gathered flowers and ate anything edible until they sampled elderberries of which there was a profusion. They were too bitter, but I explained that they could be made into elderberry syrup, an old remedy for coughs. They gathered a lot and I offered to take them home and make syrup which they could dilute and drink and they suggested we should drink it the last day before Christmas.

On the last morning of term as I stepped into the outer school door from the narrow passageway, I heard a boy's voice announce, 'Here's wor canny little teacher.' When I entered the classroom, although it was only ten minutes to nine, all the class was assembled. The desks were formed into a long oblong table covered by coloured paper and laden with plates of sandwiches, scones, mince-pies and cakes made by their mothers.

So, after the morning assembly, we ate a merry Christmas breakfast, washed down by copious drinks of diluted elderberry syrup.

Although primarily a mining community, all were interested in countryside and farming, the boys in particular helping on local farms, especially at harvest time.

That same September a particularly healthy boy was absent all week. When he returned, bronzed and vigorous, I asked why he had been absent.

'Well,' he said, 'I was going to say I had a bad cold, but now I see you I'll tell you the truth – I've been on the hay bogeys.'

That was the term when I was paid a flattering albeit amusing compliment by a boy bidding me goodbye before he left.

'It's a pity you're married, miss, because in a few years' time there's nobody I could have fancied better.'

14.

I considered carefully the specific needs of pupils in a locality such as Delaval before devising an English Syllabus, then made an outline, one which could be elaborated as seemed appropriate and this was used thereafter, 1944–1970. This may appear unambitious and dull but that was not the case. It was a fundamental from which, helped by thought and inspiration, individuality, aptitude and imagination could be developed.

Oral practice required priority: the pupils were bi-lingual, dialect predominating. I remember a boy coming in after the midday meal and saying, 'I saw a good picture last night, miss, and I want to tell you about it. Need I not talk proper?'

Dispensation received, he took off his jacket, hung it on the knob of a cupboard door and proceeded, in the vernacular, to give a graphic description of desert oil-wells and the laying of pipe lines.

Northumbrian dialect is rich in historical significance and we were later to trace dialect words back to their origins: Icelandic; Scandinavian; Norman; Germanic; Romany etc., but there were also established grammatical faults and poor enunciation. The lower jaw was lazy, speech through almost closed teeth a habit. To overcome this, we used, in odd moments, to chant jingles with one finger between the teeth. If you bit your finger you were not opening your mouth enough.

Vowels also became an off-moment relaxation – singing

AA	aa	aa.
EE	ee	ee
I	eye	eye
O	oh	oh
U	_YOU_	_YOU_

They also made up and enunciated tongue twisters.

Correcting grammar mistakes had to be done gradually, casually, and persistently, over a long time.

For instance – 'us' was used instead of 'we'.

'Whee' (pronounced 'we') meant 'Who?'.

Someone said, 'Us was goin' up Barty's Bank.'I intervened, '*We* were.'

The response was, 'Me and Tom Dixon.'

But the means by which ease was established in speaking relatively clear grammatical English was 'talks', a kind of public-speaking practice aided by the House system.

I used to give a topic once a month and everyone would prepare a two to three-minute speech in their own time. Homework was not a set feature of the school but projects such as this were done voluntarily, perhaps unwittingly, at home.

Topics I recall include: Pets I have had.

If you had to change into an animal, what would you be?

Jobs I dislike doing.

Where would you go anywhere in the world if you could?

Spending £10 today.

Buying all your Christmas presents with 6d. (this revealed much ingenuity).

I wish I could have .... included descriptions of desired possessions such as:-

the Mallard steam locomotive.

an ocean liner.

a laboratory 5'×12' with yellow walls and metal benches.

the best pigeon loft in the world.

a Jodrell Bank telescope 'because I hope to venture out into space.'

a private zoo including a white rhino.

a large yard fitted out with a hundred kennels for stray dogs.

a mansion with a square-mile garden to make into an orphanage.

a Rolls Royce Silver Cloud with a chauffeur 'to open the door'.

a private ice rink 'with lots of icicles.'

Members of one House spoke each week. A chairperson from a different House, sat at my desk to introduce the speakers, take the votes and announce the results. Someone was deputed to offer or to second a vote of thanks. Everyone voted for the talk he or she had most enjoyed.

I sat at the back of the class and each speaker knew I expected to hear every word clearly spoken. I made notes of grammatical errors and dealt with them casually, later.

In this way, three speakers were selected from each House, and entered the Finals, where they gave a speech on any subject they liked.

There was a rich and varied selection, but the one I most often recall is that where a boy talked about pigeon-rearing and racing, bringing along one of his birds for us to see. At twelve o'clock we all went outside to see the bird 'flighted' for home. Then there was a speedy departure of the entire class to see if the pigeon had arrived. I think *it* got there first.

The winner of the Final was awarded three stars, the second two, and the third one.

Pupils developed critical faculties, grumbling if anyone favoured the inferior talk of a friend.

Once a girl gave a long boring account of a film she had seen the previous evening at the small local cinema (where, incidentally, at matinees a notice was flashed on the screen, 'Please do not Pee on the floor.')

One boy voted for her and was scowled at by everyone else.

At playtime, as he drank his milk, he confided, 'I voted for her because she saved me ninepence, I was going tonight and now I don't want to see it.'

Interest always seemed to be sustained in these sessions, with satisfying consequences. When inter-school public speaking contests were inaugurated by the Rotary Club in 1961, competing, amongst others, against a large new school soon to be Comprehensive, and Blyth Grammar School, our team of three girls, Speaker, Chairman and Vote of thanks, won first prize; topic:- Our School and its Surroundings.

Over successive years we had a team gaining first, second or third prize each time.

Familiar names now appear in the local press as chairwomen, secretaries, speakers at Townswomen's Guilds and as members of Dramatic Societies.

Drama also later became a special feature of Delaval School, but that needs a separate chapter.

15.

The aim in written work was to achieve literacy – the ability to write simple English, grammatically correct, properly punctuated and accurately spelt – as well as to develop imagination.

Everyone was given a rough notebook of poor unlined paper and any work could be prepared in it. Writing could be poor, crossing-out abound, ideas could flow, be discarded or altered, but the final original work had to be transcribed neatly and correctly. As always, I regarded the final script as their manuscripts printed for publication. They exchanged books during the last week of term and read one another's stories.

Most had pride in the books, backed them with coloured paper or with designs of their own, and gave them titles. Some exist today, displayed by children as their parent's work. They contained stories, poems, articles and information, usually developed from given suggestions.

For example, I'd write on the blackboard, "I opened the door and peeped inside." Then I'd say, "door of what kind of place? I wonder what you saw. Was it beautiful? or creepy? or unusual? Write about it." This gains much better results than saying, "describe an interior." Or, I'd say, "write down a Christian name then a surname. They can be funny if you like." Then I'd put on the blackboard one of my own like "Theodora Gostick" and I'd extemporise about her. After that I'd say, "I wonder who your person is, and how she or he looks. What does she wear? What kind of voice has she? Where did you meet her? What was she doing? Do you expect to see her again? Now, write about her or him."

In a later essay we'd go on to meeting the family, which included descriptions of various types, and conversation. Sometimes an adventure, romantic or detective story developed.

A girl once filled an exercise book with the 'doings' of her imaginary family.

69

Beautiful descriptive writing could develop from a quietly spoken introduction such as:-

"Shut your eyes.
Imagine you are holding a pebble in your hand.
How does it feel? jagged? smooth? cold? etc.
How is it coloured?
Where were you when you found it?
What could you see? hear; maybe smell?
What are your thoughts or feelings about it?
What are you going to do with it.
Now write all this about it and maybe a story will grow, or a poem."

Boys liked to write full-blooded adventures, given beginnings such as "The man who was brought into camp had a diamond in his chin." A variety of stories, funny, sinister, sad and mysterious resulted from just writing 'Montmorency' on the blackboard and saying "I wonder who or what that is?"

One term we listened to the Ted Hughes *Prose and Verse* programme on the radio. We submitted a selection of work for the end of series competition and won two book tokens for the Library for poems, one by a girl Elizabeth Harrison, the other by a boy Malcolm Thompson.

However, English teaching must also meet the mundane needs of everyday life; filling in forms; giving directions; reading timetables; writing letters; so a special notebook was devoted to this aspect. The scheme was practical but always popular once underway.

First, each pupil pretended he or she had left school and was about to apply for work a considerable distance away from home. Any job could be chosen whether or not it seemed appropriate to the applicant's aptitude. Most chosen were within the range of possibility, but there was one lion-tamer, a Cousteau-like deep sea explorer and an all-in wrestler.

The initial procedure was:-
  1. Write a 'Situations Vacant' advertisement.
  2. Write a letter of application.
  3. Write to a suitable person requesting a testimonial.
  4. Write a letter of thanks for the testimonial.
  5. Write to someone asking if you may use his or her name as a reference.
You have got the job:-
  1.Write an 'Accommodation Vacant' advertisement.
  2. Write asking for details about the accommodation, remembering to enclose a stamped addressed envelope.

3. Write a reply to (2).
4. Accept the accommodation, saying you will give exact details about your arrival later.
5. Look up a bus or train timetable and write down the most suitable time for your journey to your destination.
6. Write a post-card stating the time you will arrive at your new living-place and add any other information you consider necessary.

You pack your belongings, say goodbye and leave home.

1. Write a letter home the day after your arrival describing your feelings, the journey, your new living-place, people you have met so far.
2. Letter home about your first day at work, surroundings, workmates, atmosphere etc.
3. Letter home, a week later, giving more details about work, abode, people, activities, mentioning particularly a friend you have made.
4. Letter home containing general news and views but with specific reference to a club you and your friend have joined.

It is some weeks or months later. You have been elected sports secretary at the club.

1. Write to a rival club requesting a contest.
2. Write rival club's reply giving suggested details of time, place etc.
3. Accept, on behalf of your club, corroborating, time, date and place.
4. Write a sample card suitable to send to each team member giving instructions about time, place, and any necessary gear or apparel required at the contest.
5. Write a letter home about the occasion; excitements; frustrations; personalities.

It is the end of the season and there is going to be a celebratory party.

1. Write to a restaurant, hotel or public hall to find out if a room of a suitable size is available on the date you require. Ask for a menu and how much the room and food will cost.
2. Write a reply.
3. Accept, stating any amendments or choices you require.
4. Write a formal invitation to a celebrity guest.
5. Write the celebrity's reply.
6. Write a friendly invitation to a friend.
7. Write the friend's reply.
8. Write a letter home about the party – guests; highlights; humorous incidents; dress; meal etc.

So the series continued until holidays had been selected from brochures, booking forms filled in, money suitably despatched, holiday clothes bought by post, holidays described in detail, thanks rendered for hospitality and for gifts, until finally, congratulations had to be written on promotion, engagement or marriage of a friend and condolences offered after a bereavement.

So many Delaval teenagers over the years 'lived' these letters, exposing fantasies, revealing inner yearnings, hopes and ideals. The most unexpected girls would purchase sophisticated evening attire, dance with the boss and have a subsequent speedy romance.

One boy inhabited a tenement in London with the most diverse characters, part of a rapidly changing population. A permanent boarder, however, was a 'spiv' who always took advantage of topical events and fashions to make some easy money. For example, he had everyone else in the building coaxed or coerced into making red and white and black and white favours for him, to sell outside Wembley Stadium when Manchester United played Newcastle United in the Cup Final.

In their fantasy, several boys were professional footballers. One morning I intervened in a heated argument developing between two of them. Their teams were drawn against one another; each wanted to be on the winning side. I said, "Right. It's a draw." This was accepted, but, when I read the letters later, one had a post-script: "P.S. We won the re-play."

There were ten minute Vocabulary Competitions once a week.

Punctuation was taught incidentally, and revised by occasional written exercises. I would fill a blackboard with completely unpunctuated prose and ask the class to re-write it in sentences with all the correct punctuation marks. As the content was always topical, and usually local, they were intrigued and amused by the exercise. Conversations and antics of boys and girls sitting on the area wall of the local fish and chip shop (a regular evening rendezvous) were especially popular.

I did use sets of printed comprehension exercises with Examination classes and they frequently used to grumble about having to do these. "They're dead boring." "What use are they anyway?" So one morning I took an Income Tax Form and the printed instructions on how to fill it in. I explained that in a few years time each of them would have to fill in a facsimile form, aided by the same instructions. Was their comprehension capable of this? They saw the point and completed future exercises with better grace.

As little of the money allocated to the purchase of books was used on primers and set exercises, there was a considerable amount available for general reading matter; fiction; adventure; biography; travel; nature; poetry etc. Each class had a class 'library' and librarians.

There was also a School Library, the responsibility of a member of Staff but supervised by librarians from Senior classes.

Schools had quite a liberal annual Library allowance so a wide selection of books became available over the years; as they were properly cared for they did not quickly become dilapidated.

Children like listening to stories and I read aloud to each class for fifteen or twenty minutes each week: extracts from stories, biographies, autobiographies, travel books, Readers Digests, newspaper articles, hoping to make reading a habit with them.

Sometimes they were lazy about reading themselves so questionnaires were attached to specific books and each pupil was expected to read at least two per term. As they read, or when they had completed a book, they answered the questions in written sentences, thus completing a synopsis of the content.

Each pupil was encouraged to keep a book in the desk for casual reading. Michael Flisher who had told me no one had taught him to read as he had 'always known how' used to chuckle repeatedly over Durrell's *Bafut Beagles.*

A pile of magazines was freely available. *Readers' Digest; Geographical Magazine; Good Housekeeping; The Woodworker; Amateur Gardening; Needlecraft.* Sometimes comics were added to the pile.

Work of a very simple nature was done with a class of slow-learners who were given variety and individual attention by every teacher in the school.

They enjoyed simple poetry, like James Stephens 'The Snare' and Walter de la Mare's 'Silver' and 'Nicholas Nye'. They memorised them, copied them in their poetry books and illustrated them. They liked to be awarded 'stars' for neatness and care.

They enjoyed mimes and extemporary drama, gradually developing extra detail from a basic plot or idea, bringing clothes and props from home.

I had a 'shop' with them, to combine word recognition and simple arithmetic of everyday life. Printed notices of goods for sale were displayed, all things I knew they liked. They were provided with imitation money. Each one had to recognise and write down what he or she wished to buy and give me the correct money. One boy always bought pigeons.

At first payment was easy, they only need give me actual coinage they possessed. Then, to progress, I increased the prices in such a way that no one could pay me without requiring change, and they must tell me how much change they required before I handed over their purchase (only the name printed on a slip of cardboard, but nevertheless valued).

The price of a pigeon was increased to two shillings and eightpence and I had distributed no copper. The pigeon fancier proffered three shillings. I asked, "How much change do you need?" His mind began the calculation, then his face relaxed and he said, "Oh, keep the change, miss."

His whole family was engrossed in pigeon-keeping. Once they built a wooden pen to keep them in; they completed the construction in the kitchenette, then found it was too big to be moved out of the door into the garden.

Classes such as these are by nature restive; they argue among themselves as they work.

Derek, small of stature and wiry, wanted to be a jockey when he left school. Another boy said, 'You have to be clever to be a jockey.'

'I am clever,' he replied.

'You can't read,' a girl said.

'No, I know I can't,' he agreed, 'but I'm clever.'

One day I said, 'Write down all the living things in your house; people and animals. Begin "In our house are ...." ' One boy brought me his book and I saw, 'In our house are my mother, my father, my sisters and my brother, the dog and the bugger.' I asked him to read it to me. They had a budgie (budgerigar).

16.

In 1945, the return of male teachers to their posts began and the balance of the sexes was gradually restored from its uneven wartime strength of seven women and one ineffective man.

Mr Wm Robinson, veteran and officer of two World Wars and a contemporary of Mr Soulsby's, was first to return, in July.

His Geography teaching was much superior to what mine had been during my first sojourn at Delaval, and he also taught Mathematics. He had a good relationship with the pupils: he treated boys rather like the officer ordering the troops; with the girls he was avuncular.

My mental picture is of him crossing the boys' yard purposefully and slowly at playtime, his pipe clenched between his teeth, on his way to catch boys smoking in the lavatories.

A little later, Mr Jack Chicken joined the Staff, providing the boys with opportunities for Games and Physical Education of which they had for some time been deprived.

The most progressive and virile period of Delaval school-life began in 1946 and was maintained for years thereafter.

The Log Book records that in June, 1957 the school was 'allocated a type-writer for clerical purposes' a useful amenity. But we never had a school hall, a gymnasium or a proper playing-field. The building was always what would now be regarded as completely inadequate. Sometimes, we had to put buckets and baths in the long corridor to catch rain coming through the roof until the colliery workmen came to mend it. There were only outside lavatories for children and staff.

But we had a dedicated Headmaster, a loyal industrious Staff and pupils proud of their school, eager to maintain good standards in work, play and inter-relationships.

The school became known for its happy hospitable atmosphere.

One HMI, visiting a Berwick school, where a former Blyth man was Head-master, said, 'You belong to Blyth? That is where Delaval, the friendly school is.'

Its achievements in Games and Athletics, and its successes in Drama were reported regularly in the local Press. Its originality, versatility, and the way in which everyone in the school became involved in its activities, were repeatedly commended. On three occasions we gained the prestige of commendatory paragraphs in the *Daily Mail* and *Daily Mirror*.

My husband returned from India at the end of December, 1945, was demobi-lised from the RAF a few weeks later, resuming his duties at Delaval on 1st March, 1946.

This added immediate strength to the school. Although academically trained at Hulme Grammar School and St Luke's College, Exeter, he was, at heart, a craftsman and had considerable personal skill in various crafts. He had gained extra teaching qualifications in Woodwork and Metalwork. He was a keen and knowledgeable gardener and had been Athletics Captain at school and college.

He expected and maintained disciplined behaviour and good standards of work, but encouraged originality. Woodwork tools were checked at the end of every lesson. Gardening tools and boots had to be cleaned and put away in their appointed places. I sometimes told him he exacted a greater tidiness than he practised himself at home. No one was expected to 'down tools' in the middle of a task because a bell had announced the end of the afternoon session. There was some resentment about this at times but it was off-set by the pleasure the boys had in making sledges, fishing reels etc., for their own use and presents for their relatives and friends.

They developed a pride in the garden and would inspect their Class plots in a proprietary way. Several became farmworkers and professional gardeners: one became Head Park-keeper in a Yorkshire town, another at Ridley Park, Blyth. Many work yet as joiners and carpenters, one or two with small businesses of their own. One boy became apprentice of the year at a Tyne shipyard, one technical adviser for Northern England for a well known kitchen-fitment firm.

No further previous members of Staff returned. Instead young enthusiastic men, trained sometimes after War Service, joined us. In these, too, Delaval was fortunate, for they all gave dedication and skill to their work, becoming de-voted to the well-being of the school and giving much of their own free time to its extra-mural pursuits.

I shall mention some individually, hereafter, because of the special contribution they made to the life of the school, but I have for all of them an affectionate regard and always appreciated their attitude towards me. They showed, at all times, loyalty and respect, accepted any authority I needed to show with goodwill and sought my approval and opinion of their projects. I am happy still to number them, and their wives and families, among my personal friends.

Their special academic attainments were of a sufficiently wide range to enable good specialist teaching to be offered in each subject on the timetable; but, even more important, was the contribution they made to the community life of the school, particularly in Games, Athletics and Drama.

By 1947 the girls became the more deprived sex as married women teachers left to resume household duties or become mothers. They still had the advantage of good specialist teaching in Domestic Science and Needlework but no one to was available for Physical Education. This meant there was no one to coach netball, rounders or athletics, to enable them to participate in inter-school competitions.

This seemed unfair as well as unfortunate, because they were eager to compete for the Inter-school Netball Shield and to take part in the Blyth Schools Athletics Meeting.

I had no athletic ability. The only event I had ever won as a schoolgirl was an obstacle race, and that was because I was so small and thin I could wriggle under tarpaulins and through hoops with comparative ease and I am tenacious by nature. Nevertheless, I could give encouragement, and coach to some extent 'from the book'. I volunteered to give up two junior English classes and supervise Physical Education in the time this made available.

The success of this enterprise in the normal way would have been doubtful, but circumstances favoured us.

In 1947 Mr R Butterworth joined the Staff as Science Master, followed in 1948 by Mr J Bennington (Maths) and Mr J A N Pollard (English); all young enthusiastic and dedicated. Each was duly appointed to a House. In this year also, Mr Soulsby presented to the school the Soulsby Sports Trophy for inter-house competition in football, netball and athletics. Friendly rivalry became keen.

My husband had always been particularly interested in athletics. Sets of hurdles were constructed in the Woodwork classes, javelins and shot requisitioned from the PE allocation and there was always a plentiful supply of footballs, netballs, cricket and rounders gear. High jump stands and bars were kept in good repair by the boys.

Girls and boys practised athletics together during the lunch break and after school in the afternoon. My husband coached hurdling, starting and short runs. Mr Bennington and Mr Pollard supervised javelin throwing, putting the shot, and long-distance and cross-country running. Everyone coached 'passing the baton'. Running 'up the Laverick' became more popular than walking.

In girls' PE and Games lessons I did the best I could technically, refereed netball practices and matches after school, and accompanied the team on all away occasions. I did foster appreciation of fair play and the need to show a good spirit in competition.

Men and boys came to netball matches; women and girls went to football matches. There was much enthusiasm but no rowdyism.

I recall with affection odd incidents

Mr Soulsby had great faith in vitamins, so before netball matches he used to dose the team with rosehip syrup, Ribena and vitamin B tablets.

My insistence on clean fair play was occasionally undermined. One afternoon, I overheard the team captain, a tall strong quiet girl who later married a clergyman, saying, as we walked to a match, 'Play fair; but if *they* kick, you kick, and if *they* shove, you shove.' At that point I intervened.

On another occasion, as we walked to the local RC school, great protagonists, a member of the team said, 'I've been praying all the afternoon that we'll win.'

I said, 'So if St Wilfred's team has been praying equally hard, will it be a draw?'

I later tried to explain that to pray that you will play as well as you possibly can is a better idea.

Only once did a fight break out at a netball match and that was at St Wilfred's, between two boys, one from each school.

When I intervened, Eddie told me he had been fighting because the other lad had said I was skinny. I said 'Well, I am, so wait until someone calls me Fatty before you get annoyed.'

Over the years, the combined efforts of Staff and pupils were well rewarded. The boys won the Hyde Inter-school Football Shield in 1948. The girls won the Inter-school Athletics Challenge Shield in 1952.

The school was represented in the Northumberland County Schools Athletics Team by at least one athlete every year from 1948 to 1953, and for three successive years produced the Northumbrian Junior Girls' Hurdling champion.

A newspaper cutting in my album mentions Jean Childs going to the All England Championships at Southampton in 1951 and Marion Douglass to Bradford in 1952.

Yet our school population was small compared with that of other schools and we still had no gymnasium, no hall, no playing-field of our own. Nor had we any feeling of rancour or deprivation. We were a happy school.

My timetabled Physical Education lessons were unorthodox and disapproved of by one County Organizer although others were helpful and understanding.

This particular one recommended that I should attend a Teaching Gymnastics Course, which was to take place one evening each week for six consecutive weeks at Gosforth.

I declined, but she became rather awkward, doubtless sensing my antagonism. Finally, she said, 'I'm sure someone could be found to teach PE here properly who could teach English too.' I decided to go to the first session.

I went in a decidedly unco-operative mood, not even attempting to wear suitable attire. The session included rope-climbing, horse-vaulting and work on parallel bars; I sat and took no part.

At the end of the evening I went across and said to the organizer and the instructor, 'At the school where I teach we have no rope, no horse, no parallel bars, nor any other gymnastic equipment. And, if we had, there is no hall to put them in, and, in any case, I am physically incapable of demonstrating their use, so I shall not be coming to any further sessions.'

Later, we did acquire a vaulting-horse and forms which were used in the playgrounds, or in the long corridor by the boys in wet weather.

If it was icy or snowy, I took the girls for walks or runs 'up the Laverick' and allowed them to slide and have snowball-fights.

If it was wet, we moved all the desks in my classroom to the sides and extemporised exercises to music, making up a kind of Dance-Drama or Movement to Music which became quite popular.

On fine days they performed various exercises and activities, and played netball, tennis or rounders in the girls' playground.

I have happy memories of sunny days, the girls playing a game wholeheartedly whilst larks sang incessantly above, and I tried to keep my mind on what was happening.

I remember two colliery workmen sitting one whole morning on the roof, which they were supposed to be repairing, watching a succession of girls' classes. It embarrassed me, as such attention made me feel even more inadequate.

As I walked into school at the end of the morning one of them came over and said, 'You have a nice cushie job miss.'

Tennis in the forties was not a popular game with boys in our area; they regarded it as effeminate and elitist.

Mr Butterworth, however, was a good tennis player and he began lunch-hour coaching so that it soon became popular. We were able to use the courts in the grounds of the Miners' Welfare Park. Eventually, there were occasional Staff v School doubles contests during the last hour on a Friday afternoon.

I was always an interested onlooker, but no one ever saw me attempting to play. My husband said I held a tennis racket as if it were a frying-pan. Someone else thought I should have a retriever dog to collect all the balls I missed.

At one of the Staff v School afternoons, a colleague heard a girl say, 'Why does Mrs Wrigley never play?'

Her companion replied, 'Oh, I expect she's too good at it.'

Thus is fame falsely acquired.

17.

Drama, which eventually became a dominant feature of school-life, had an inauspicious beginning. Early in 1948, Mr Soulsby suggested an innovation to the timetable.

Formal lessons should be dispensed with for the second half of each Friday afternoon, and each teacher should inaugurate a 'Club' devoted to a specific hobby or activity. Pupils would be free, as far as feasible, to attend the club of their choice, remaining in it for at least one complete term.

The choices offered included Chess, Photography, (Mr Soulsby bought a school camera), Art, Cookery, Needlework and Handicrafts, Nature and Drama. I found myself with a Drama Club of sixty members.

Initially, we did 'free' acting, mime etc., but I felt a Drama Club should produce a public performance of some sort and wanted everyone to take an active part.

Printed plays considered were either over-ambitious or had too few parts, so I decided to devise an entertainment of song and drama.

Miss Hargreaves, the Music teacher, agreed to join me in running the Drama Club and we constructed a suitable programme.

She rehearsed the entire cast in local folk songs, such as *Waters of Tyne* and *Bobby Shaftoe*. *The Lambton Worm* was performed in song and mime. An episode from local history, a blood-curdling piece of folk-lore 'The Long Pack' was enacted.

Finally, as light relief, I wrote a humorous sketch in dialect about topical events in the life of two typical mining families. This was the first of what became known locally as 'the Delaval plays'. That was over thirty years ago and I cannot even remember its title, although I have the manuscripts of three later sketches.

This programme, the Drama Club gradually built-up and rehearsed over successive Friday afternoons until the end of the summer term was approaching. Costumes were improvised by parents or made by members of the Needlework Club.

Then Mr Soulsby hired the Delaval Miners' Welfare Hall, (originally an Army hut) for the evening of July 21st and the officials allowed us to use it two afternoons for dress rehearsals. Tickets were sold to parents and friends. It was only during the second full dress rehearsal, on the actual day of the performance, that I realized we should have had stage sets. There was suitable furniture on the stage, but just bare surrounds with performers waiting in the wings in full view, and no special stage-lighting.

We tried to improvise with screens covered by newspapers and hastily distempered, but they were quite ineffective. They looked a mess. Otherwise, this first concert was a success, according to our kind and uncritical audience, and we were encouraged to prepare another entertainment for the following Christmas.

By then, the Drama Club had greater expertise because Mr J A N Pollard joined the Staff in August that year and became co-producer. He had taken an active part in amateur theatricals and knew how to tackle all the things of which I was ignorant: stage-craft; lighting; make-up etc.

'What Cheer, Delaval', as the variety concert was advertised had much more polish and sophistication than our first effort.

For it, Mr Soulsby hired the hall of St Bede's church, Newsham, because it was larger than the Newsham Miners' Welfare and had a much better stage with entrances and exits at each side. Placing sixty on it at once for the finale still required considerable manoeuvring.

Everyone took part in a simple presentation of the Nativity, in song and verse. The Christmas Sunday School story from 'Mrs Wiggs in the Cabbage Patch' was dramatized. The second Delaval play, 'The Christmas Draw', about the same two mining families was presented. Everyone, Drama Club members and audience joined in carol-singing.

Again, we had a kind appreciative audience on both evenings, and the enthusiasm of the Drama Club increased. We soon had a long waiting-list for membership which we were unable to reduce except when members reached the statutory age and left school. Eventually, we were importuned to run an Old Scholars Drama Club too.

The second 'What Cheer, Delaval' concert was given in St Bede's Hall on July 12th and 13th, 1949. An innovation was a guest artiste each evening.

Mr T Aldus, a popular local conjuror, delighted his young audience on the Tuesday evening. On the Wednesday, we had with us Archie Armstrong, a popular folk-singer and raconteur who frequently broadcast from the BBC Studio in Newcastle. He sang, told anecdotes, and compèred the whole programme.

For it, I devised a pageant described by the local press as 'a representation in verse and song of the history of Northumberland from the time of the ancient Britons, through the eras of St Cuthbert and William the Conqueror, to Grace Darling and George Stephenson.' Incidentally, it was William the Conqueror who gave the area of land on which our school was built to Guy de la Val (Delaval).

One group of players enacted *The Elsdon Murder* the tale of William Winter, a gipsy who was hanged on the gibbet on the moors near Elsdon where a wooden representation of his skull still hangs, the scene making an eerie silhouette at twilight against the starkness of its sombre background.

Finally, the Delaval play, about the same two mining families, *Buying a Pup*. This was published locally soon afterwards and performed by Youth Clubs and small Drama groups in Northumberland and Durham over ensuing years.

The Pantomime Era

1950 marked the beginning of the Pantomime era, which lasted until I retired in 1970.

Although always referred to as pantomimes by successive years of pupils and the local populace, they were really stories in which the dialogue was interspersed with songs and dances which helped to develop or emphasise the plot. 'Good' always eventually overcame 'Evil', in personified form, the successful denouement was always engineered by a band of mischievous Delaval children, and as our membership had increased, there had always to be a place for at least seventy youngsters. Good actors and actresses had the more ambitious parts but they were not necessarily the most academic pupils; we found some quite unexpected talent. But there were numerous characters, or groups of characters, with one or two lines to say, little groups to dance, and everyone sang.

Dramatically and artistically, adverse criticism could have been levelled. A drama teacher from a neighbouring school who attended the first show told Mr Soulsby afterwards that there were far too many people on the stage and not enough opportunity given to our few good performers, which was probably true. But the pantomimes did something more important: they bound us all, staff and pupils, into a corporate whole in which disparate intellectual and social distinctions went unnoticed.

As the time for each annual production approached, it became the focal point of school-life. The cast rehearsed during lunch breaks and after school. Materials were bleached, dyed and laundered in the domestic science room. The Needlework Club, augmented by interested parents, made costumes of original design. Boys in the woodwork room made sets and props. The Art Club did the painting and in this we were particularly fortunate, as we had the services of an itinerant Art teacher, Mr Wilf Hardy, who came to the school two days each week. He had been a commercial artist before taking up teaching and still did freelance work, especially cartoons. No permanent member of Staff could have been more happily involved than he. He painted beautiful 'Shoe' houses, under-water scenes, horses, ocean-liners and desert-isles with equal ease. Once, when we found ourselves short of a window curtain at the last moment, he took paints, brushes and paper and produced what appeared to be a length of intricately-patterned cretonne in a few minutes.

Mr Bennington was in charge of ticket sales, and helped by a selection of volunteer boys, devised and worked the stage lighting.

There was never a shortage of willing stage-hands and always a music librarian.

After a time a printing-press and sets of type were acquired, and, under Miss Hargreaves' direction, the tickets and programmes were printed.

Mr Soulsby was enthusiastic all the time and solicitous about the health of all, with Ribena and vitamin B tablets always to hand.

There really was total involvement, and there is seldom a chance meeting with past pupils without pantomime incidents figuring prominently in the 'do you remembers'.

When I was purchasing new shoes recently, the assistant said, 'Do you remember how hard I found it to get the steps right in the Fire Dance? I used to keep glancing into the wings so you could keep me right.' That must have been more than twenty years ago.

Babes in Humford Woods

The first pantomime was 'Babes in Humford Woods'.

The original Babes in the Wood story formed a skeletal plot: the woods on the banks of the River Blyth, where Delaval youngsters spent much of their free time, was the setting.

The Baron of Humford, who was always doing mis-spelt crosswords and filling in football coupons because he wanted cash to enable him to escape from his domineering Baroness, had to take care of his dead brother's two children, the Babes. Hoping to inherit the money left to the Babes by their father, he hired two Villains to waylay them and drown them in the swimming-pool at Humford Baths.

But one Villain was exceedingly superstitious and refused to drown the Babes on the day they waylaid them, after reading horoscopes in the daily newspaper.

The first Villain was born on November 5th and the horoscope for that birthdate read, 'today is a bad day for carrying out business transactions.' The second Villain was born on April 1st and he was advised, 'to keep away from water and beware of carrying out big projects.' So they decided to tie the Babes to a tree until the following day which might prove more propitious. Whilst they were roping the Babes, the Kids from the Oval with their dog Jet, 'a great long-legged lurcher' arrived on the scene, and grabbed the Villains. They told the Babes to run and find Robin Hood 'and his Missus' who would help them. Then the Kids tied the Villains to a tree.

The Babes, soon lost, lay down under a tree, robins came, danced gently around them, covering them with leaves and sang a lullaby. Then there was a Nursery Rhymes Dance Sequence for the Babes' happy dream.

Eventually, due to the united efforts of Robin Hood, Maid Marian, Friar Tuck, outlaws and their ladies, King, Queen, lords, ladies and the Kids from the Oval with their dog, the Babes were rescued and the Baron and Villains brought to justice.

The Baron was sentenced to spend the rest of his days with the Baroness and never send in another football coupon.

The Villain with new false teeth had to eat large quantities of brazil nuts every day.

The superstitious Villain had to say 'Pig!' a hundred times a day with his thumbs tied securely down and to keep walking under a ladder at the same time.

The finale was a sing-song around a camp-fire in the woods.

Music ranged from 'Daddy wouldn't buy me a bow-wow' and 'I wouldn't leave my little wooden hut for you' to Grainger's 'Country Gardens'. It also included four songs composed by Mr Pollard, who couldn't read music, but having made up the words devised a tune by whistling. When he had achieved a melody which satisfied him, he whistled it to Miss May Hargreaves, who picked it out on the piano, then wrote it down and arranged an accompaniment.

This procedure JAN Pollard described himself in the following parody. With Apologies to Alfred Noyes.

"He read not a note of music, ('tis said that he did not try)
But he shouldered his burden bravely and managed to just scrape by;
He whistled a tune to the piano, and who should be sitting there,
But the poor old music teacher,
May, the music teacher,
Knocking out pseudo song-hits into the startled air."

JANP

Nevertheless, the Villains' rollicking, 'If you want any dirty work done, send for us!' Maid Marian's plaintive 'Sitting by the fire and dreaming,' and the Outlaws rousing, 'Here we live beneath the greenwood tree' were all melodious, and were whistled or sung around Delaval School and its environs long after the pantomime was over.

Costuming the show required ingenuity as we had little cash in the school fund and there was still an aftermath of wartime shortage of materials. However, the needlework teacher, Miss Horn, managed to purchase an old RAF parachute which provided yards of good silk. I shall always remember seeing Mrs Jessie Mowatt, the Domestic Science teacher, her hands one day almost blistered by Domestos used to bleach the silk and stained various colours on subsequent days as she dyed pieces to greenwood green, robin red and brown etc. My scrap-book contains pictures of the Needlework Club girls stitching diligently.

My mother used to say she always came twice to our shows, once to enjoy the performance and again to see how much clothing belonging to her was on the stage.

Treasured properties which appeared in the finale of shows over the years were a silk topper and long-tailed frock coat. The top hat, donated by a parent, was in pristine condition, still in its original box. The frock coat had been worn with considerable reluctance by my husband as best man at a friend's wedding. He gladly donated it to the Drama Club wardrobe.

For the actual presentation of 'Babes in Humford Woods' Mr Soulsby had hired the Miners' Welfare Hall at Blyth which had a seating capacity of 350, for March 6th, 8th and 13th 1950, but the demand for tickets was such that he had to add a further evening.

The total audience exceeded 1,000 and the *Newcastle Journal* commended the quality of 'a performance rehearsed by a cast of seventy in a room 24 feet by 21 feet'. We even earned a report of about 100 words in the Daily Mirror under the heading, 'Panto – broadly speaking.'

Pantomimes were an exhausting, albeit exhilarating experience for the Staff, consuming much time and energy, and normal school activities and studies had to be maintained. At the end of each final performance, as scenery was removed, costumes folded and packed, make-up trays checked and tidied, and mislaid property searched for, I would stand on the stage, usually clutching a beautiful bouquet, feeling a sense of release and rather delicious emptiness. And, almost inevitably, some small character, maybe a robin, a demon or a rabbit, would approach shyly and say, 'Miss, what is the next pantomime going to be?'

Well, the next pantomime was 'The Old Woman Who Lived in a Shoe' and took place in December of the same year – 1950, the only time we produced two in one year.

Delaval School outing to Etal and Ford

New Delaval County Modern School Staff
Top: J. Mowatt, J. Bennington, J. Pollard, R. Butterworth.
Bottom: R. Crossland, E. M. Hargreaves, W. Robinson, S. Soulsby, R. Wrigley, L. Wrigley, E. Horn.

New Delaval athletics practice

Presentation to Mr Soulsby on his retirement as Headmaster of New Delaval Senior School (copyright)

'The lost Totem' (copyright)

18.

The Old Woman Who Lived in a Shoe.

To justify the use of three teachers for the Drama Club, we felt it necessary to increase the membership to ninety, about a third of the school. First-year pupils had, perforce, to be ineligible.

To meet the needs of so large a cast dual plots seemed advisable, a humorous one helping a romantic one to a successful denouement.

'The Old Woman Who Lived in a Shoe' had three stage sets: Shoe Village; the exterior of Mealy Castle; a Woodland Glade.

Two 'shoe' houses were set against a rural background.

The larger one, inhabited by the Old Woman, Nasturtium, the Old Man, Accumulator, and their nine children, was a pit boot. The smaller one, more elegant, was the home of Mother Hubbard and her dog Winkle, which was constantly begging for a bone, a good supply of which his owner always kept in her Shoe cupboard alongside other delicious eatables.

The Old Man spent all his days going around with a sack picking up anything which he thought might come in handy. I could never convince my husband that I had not modelled Accumulator on him. In a later show, Mr Soulsby was convinced that he was my inspiration for Miss Constance Poorly, who took her medicine chest as well as her gramophone to a desert isle, but, as I assured them, any similarity to real people was entirely accidental.

At Mealy Castle, King Hannibal Hercules Huge lived with his Queen Persilla and their lovely gentle daughter, Monacella, whose unwilling betrothal to Prince Bartholomew Bulky was being announced at the beginning of the play.

For the occasion, Queen Persilla wore her real crown instead of the imitation one she usually used, and was scolded by her husband when he realized this, because it contained a large diamond with which he hoped to purchase huge amounts of food at a future date.

91

Perturbed by her husband's rage and her daughter's unhappiness the Queen stumbled as she went up the Castle steps and the crown fell off. It was picked up by her maid Sylvia and restored to the Queen's head without either of them noticing the diamond had fallen out. It was picked up casually, along with other odds and ends, by the Old Man, as he passed the Castle with his sack.

Monacella decided she could not bear life with a Prince as fat and gluttonous as her father, and ran away alone to a remote woodland glade.

There she was befriended by rabbits, birds and butterflies which guarded her from the malevolence of a Demon aided by a band of bats, beetles and flies.

Woodlanders and villagers came to the glade as they searched for someone to be crowned May Queen for the May festival at which the Lord of the Land opened his palace grounds for their festivities.

The Old Woman's children came to the glade as the Old Man had decided to open 'Boot Castle' to the public, at sixpence a visit, and had told them to go far and wide to announce this. When they saw Monacella looking pale and hungry they decided they would fetch her some food if they could find any and Laggy said he would like to give her 'something pretty' too. They set off for Shoe Village.

The woodlanders decided Monacella would be a perfect May Queen.

The Lord of the Land entered the glade with his Huntsman, approved their choice, gave Monacella the glade as a sanctuary for herself and the animals, and wished he could marry her.

Back at Boot Castle, the children rummaged the Old Man's sacks for food, without success and decided they would have to 'borrow' some from Mother Hubbard's cupboard. Laggy had found the diamond in a sack and as it seemed 'something pretty' for Monacella he put it in his pocket. When Mother Hubbard came home and went to get a bone for Winkle 'the cupboard was bare, and so the poor dog got none'. She wanted to find the culprits.

Eventually, King Hannibal Hercules Huge, promised to give anything to get the diamond, his iron rations, back. So Laggy gave the Lord of the Land the diamond and he claimed Monacella as his bride for handing it back to its royal owner.

Everyone attended the wedding feast in the glade to eat, dance and sing.

Nasturtium was given a large tin of boot polish and new green laces for her house.

Accumulator became a Civil Servant to Santa Claus, filling sacks with children's letters which he intended to copy in triplicate and file in due course.

The preparations for this show involved hard work and much ingenuity, and its success was due as much to the dressing and staging as to the performance itself.

The Boot and Shoe, with suitable doors, windows and steps, were made in the Woodwork Room and decorated beautifully by Mr Hardy, helped by members of the Art Club. Caves, standing trees, rocks and a castle backcloth were also constructed and painted.

Special lighting devices, for sunshine and shade, and for 'good' and 'evil' portent were devised by Mr Bennington.

The costuming was splendid. The receipts from 'Babes in Humford Woods' had left a considerable sum in the school fund even after new 'kit' had been bought for netball and football teams and a day-out for the whole school subsidised. Cheap, colourful oddments of material were bought in bulk from a stall on Blyth market.

Art, Needlework and Domestic Science classes evolved striking, symbolic costumes for bats, beetles, butterflies, rabbits etc. When they danced their 'good' versus 'evil' ballet-style sequences, to music from *Peer Gynt*, the scene was entrancing.

Interested parents and relatives of the Staff helped too, so the comic costumes and children's clothes were mostly improvised from garments loaned or donated. Winkle, was enclosed in someone's old fur coat, suitably adjusted to dog style. This became another valued 'prop'.

The week before the actual presentation of 'The Old Woman' the timetable was abandoned entirely for each afternoon session. Every child in the school and each member of Staff was involved in some way in the production.

Finishing touches were being put to scenery and last-minute props devised.

Costumes were being completed, laundered if necessary, pressed, labelled and packed.

Type for the programme was set up and about 500 copies printed, dried and tied in bundles. Tickets ebbed and flowed and money was collected. Mr Bennington finished technical devices for the lighting and watched a rehearsal so that he could insert lighting-cues in his script.

Scenery and props had to be transported to the Miners' Welfare Hall at Blyth, two miles away, and fixed in position.

We were all at the Miners' Welfare Hall for two dress-rehearsals that week; otherwise all rehearsing was done in a classroom with overspill in the corridor.

At these last rehearsals some performers were tense, many anxious, a few over-ebullient; all were excited. Lines were forgotten, entrances missed; there was frustration and annoyance. Mr Soulsby moved from one area to another always cool, always cheerful, with a gift for establishing calm.

We had to make rotas of programme-sellers, ushers and usherettes, as so many offered their services. My husband had a stalwart band of volunteer stage hands.

Then came the opening night with make-up to apply to ninety excited youngsters. A friendly chemist had mixed for us a huge bottle of suntan make-up for girls' legs and woodlanders' arms. Wives and women teachers made-up the girls' faces and helped with head-dresses etc. Mr Pollard did all the speciality make-up. I made-up normal boys' faces under his direction, a very simple procedure once I had overcome their initial distaste for wearing make-up at all. Thereafter, I had to keep a wary eye on the box so that no unauthorised beards or moustaches would appear on the stage.

The cast had to be restrained from peeping out of the dressing-rooms' doors or between the curtains as the audience began to mount the stairs.

The orchestra took its place: the pianist Miss Hargreaves, a violinist friend, Mr Fred Taylor and a past scholar Ivan Barrass, who was later to become a professional drummer of some calibre, but who always, throughout ensuing years loyally gave us his services for 'pantomime week'.

Then came 'God Save the King', hall-lights dimmed, spot-lights picked out the stage, I gave the signal for the curtains to open and the show was on.

There were Press notices variously titled: 'School panto written by teacher', 'Teachers write songs for school panto'. (Mr Pollard and Miss Hargreaves had collaborated to produce two tuneful numbers, 'In the Springtime' and 'There's a Boy for every Girl') – 'Scholars' Panto a Winner'.

Here is a brief extract from the last one:-

"There was a capacity audience for this closing performance of a highly successful run and the children were applauded for their show. With a cast of more than 80, the show was played with zest from the opening curtain to the finale, and the numerous songs plus a strong dash of humour, kept up the promise of the opening scenes. Whilst the parts allotted to some people gave them more chance to shine than others, all played with spirit and were obviously sorry that Thursday's show was the last."

The proceeds of one extra performance were given to the National Children's Orphanage as a tribute to Buchanan.

It was in this same school year that New Delaval Modern School Old Scholars' Association was inaugurated, with an initial membership of 120.

Officials and committee were elected, social evenings and sports competitions reviewed and a Drama Section organized. The latter flourished and survived over a period of years, with a membership of thirty-two. Ages ranged from fourteen to twenty. We were allowed the use of a classroom by the Education Authority, lighting and heating free, so there were no running expenses.

Officially, the session was 7 pm to 9 pm, but members strolled in anytime between 6.30 pm and 8 pm, and it was often almost ten o'clock before everyone had departed to the local fish and chip shop. I used to accept a selection of single chips from the open paper packets proffered as I passed gossiping groups on my way to the bus-stop.

We had the use of the school table-tennis table in the corridor and the school record player. They provided their own records.

Miss Hargreaves played the piano and members sang and danced.

Mr Pollard and I directed impromptu acting.

Soon they were requesting material for a public performance, and, as nearly every member had been a principal in one school production or another, there was real talent available. We began rehearsal of a Northumbrian evening on the old 'What cheer, Geordie' lines, including a new Delaval sketch, 'Nature Cure' in 1950, and presented it in St Bede's Hall to a capacity audience.

Spurred by this success, Drama Club members, urged me to make a pantomime for them, so I promised to attempt a script for the following year.

Other events mark this particular year in my scrapbook.

Mr Soulsby decided to have a different kind of Speech Day from the usual verbose occasion, one with a minimum of formality and something to interest everyone. For it, he had booked the Plaza Cinema at Newsham, a small place, but close to the school and with more seating accommodation than St Bede's Hall. He thought he might as well make use of the screen too.

There were three keen, competent amateur photographers on the Staff, himself, my husband, and Mr Ron Butterworth, who, at the time of writing, is President of Leicester Photographic Society, gives lectures on the subject and has won national and international awards. From their combined collection of colour slides an assortment was selected and an imaginary journey planned.

At the end of the official procedure Mr Soulsby showed the slides with his own commentary, projecting Austria, Scotland, Northumberland in general, but Blyth in particular – market and harbour scenes – and finally the school itself, our own 'ancient monument'.

It was on this Speech Day, too, that the school song, 'Never Despair', was first heard in public.

Mr Soulsby knew our numbers could be depleted, unless official circumstances were altered, on the completion of a new comprehensive school, and we already had fewer pupils than rival schools, a handicap in competitive sports especially. He had several times expressed a wish for a stirring school song which would express defiance of difficulties.

One afternoon, as I was travelling by bus to Newcastle, the words drifted into my mind and I scribbled them down in the back of a diary. Later, I transcribed them and gave them to Miss Hargreaves, who composed a rousing tune and gave Mr Soulsby the completed manuscript for his approval.

He was delighted. He was so proud of it and thereafter he always stood to attention for it as for 'God Save the King' and expected everyone else to do likewise. It was amusing to see visitors, especially unfamiliar dignitaries on the platform, not sure whether to stand up or sit down.

It was popular with the school and could be heard whistled 'up the Laverick', sung from the fish and chip shop wall and vociferously rendered on return bus trips along with 'Ten Green Bottles', 'Guide me, oh thou great Jehovah', and 'She'll be coming round the Mountain when she comes'.

The *Blyth News* gave an account of this Speech Day, referring to New Delaval Secondary Modern School as 'a local school with a difference, which is known for the initiative of its staff'.

It included the chorus and verse of 'Never Despair', the School Song.

Chorus: Never despair, put forth your best endeavour
In work or play, whatever chance befall;
Never despair; with head and heart forever
Strive on, 'gainst odds, for pride of Delaval.

Verse: We will not faint, nor fail, for lack of number,
The first essential is the will to win;
No drawback shall our faith and aim encumber;
Never despair! defeated, once again begin.

I recall this Speech Day as a particularly friendly occasion, its cordial atmosphere contributed to by the Chairman, Alderman Gilbert Barker, later to be Mayor of Blyth several times, a Delaval man himself and always a loyal supporter of the school, and his wife, a lady of sweetness and courage, who presented the prizes.

In 1951, there were no Drama Club productions, although we rehearsed 'Another Sleeping Beauty' conscientiously, in readiness for presentation early in 1952.

The 'Old Scholars' prepared their first pantomime with unhurried enjoyment and gave a variety concert in aid of the Wesleyan Chapel where Mr Soulsby was an active member.

In this year also, the school choir, trained by Miss Hargreaves and conducted by Mr Soulsby, won third prize in the hymn-singing contest at the Wansbeck Musical Festival.

On July 12th, hired buses paid for by pantomime funds, took the whole school on a day's outing.

The First Year went to Cragside, near Rothbury, now a National Trust property, but at that time, the home of the Armstrong family. In 1863, Sir W G Armstrong, head of the renowned armaments works on Tyneside, built a mansion on a plateau of a steep boulder-strewn heather-clad slope, overlooking the River Coquet. He terraced the slopes, planted a variety of trees and flowering shrubs and made carriage-ways and steep winding paths to the summit where there are two artificial lakes made by damming the Black Burn.

The grounds are open to the public and provide ample space and freedom for youngsters to enjoy themselves among the trees and by the lakes. The scent and colour of the azaleas and rhododendrons in late spring and early summer are memorable, whilst the panoramic view from the top is spectacular at all times.

The seniors' outing was more formally educational, viewing the lower reaches of the Aln and the Coquet, visiting Alnwick Castle and Warkworth Castle.

I recall two particular incidents. We were conducted round Alnwick Castle by a knowledgeable but rather dour guide. Everyone was impressed by the splendid rooms and their contents; the boys especially interested in the armoury with its guns, lances, swords, halberds etc., arranged in geometric designs around the walls. But, in the long drawing-room framed autographed letters from Royalty attracted more attention than the furnishings, with the exception of the big fireplace with its high ornate surround.

One girl surveyed it carefully and then remarked to the guide, 'The Duchess must be a tall woman if she can see to comb her hair in that mirror.'

This drew only an unsmiling, 'Ladies *never* comb their hair in the drawing-room.'

We reached Warkworth in late afternoon and inspected the lay-out of the ruined castle, then let everyone free to play on the grass, hire boats on the river, or wander up the steep street of the old place buying ice-cream and presents.

The Staff went into a café for eagerly awaited cups of tea. Too soon, there was a sudden sharp shower. Two of us went out to round up the wanderers and send them back to the buses. The boats were tied up empty, the river green deserted, only a few stragglers in the street. But, in the church was a long queue at the visitors' book. They had already almost completed a page.

The only pantomime presented at Delaval that year was at the Christmas party, and I mention it because it typifies the relaxed atmosphere of the school and the friendliness which existed between Staff and pupils without loss of respect or discipline.

Mr Pollard suggested that we should end the evening with a Staff pantomime which he would write and produce.

It was a version of 'Babes in the Wood', had no music; was in rhymed couplets and lasted ten minutes.

Miss Horn, short of stature and rotund, with a round beaming face, was the Demon King, behorned and in scarlet blouse and pantaloons. Mr Crossland, a newcomer who had at once become a staunch 'Delavalite', was Fairy Queen, with gilded crown, glittering wand and dark moustache, in a calf-length frilly crepe paper frock, smoking a pipe and dancing in his frog-flippers. Messrs Bennington and Pollard, both six·feet plus and the latter with a bushy fair moustache, were the Babes, one wearing Austrian leder-hosen and the other a large replica of a little girl's frock.

Mr Hardy was the wicked Baron and made meticulous preparations, including painting a family portrait, complete with cravat, wicked twirly moustache and rosy nose, to hang in the baronial hall. Its gilded cardboard frame looked three-dimensional. We hung it above the Staff-room fireplace afterwards where it remained for several years.

Miss Hargreaves and my husband were the hired villains, suitably attired in peaked caps and eye patches.

Mr Soulsby was the police-sergeant who rescued the Babes and arrested the villains assisted by a constable – all five feet of me in an extemporised uniform and a cardboard helmet. Mr Soulsby decided he was going to appear authentically-clad and arranged to borrow the uniform of a real police-sergeant of his acquaintance for an hour. It was much too big for him in every way.

The hilarity of the assembled school reached its peak when he appeared on the stage. The fact that he had completely forgotten the two couplets he was supposed to speak went quite unnoticed. They would never have been heard above the enthusiastic applause he received.

Next morning, there was the usual respectful silence as he entered to take assembly, and classroom relationships were back to normal, mirthful reminiscing confined to the mid-morning milk break.

19.

Our sabbatical year, drama-wise, had not been wasted; much basic work having been done for 'Another Sleeping Beauty', and it was ready for presentation on five evenings in mid-February, 1952.

This was to be the last opportunity for Dick Parkin to amuse the audience as 'fat man' for it was his last term at school. He was a tall, stalwart, broad-built lad, but not roly-poly fat. Nevertheless, with padded costumes and pillow-belly, he looked immense. By chance, he had been cast as Friar Tuck, but King Hannibal Hercules Huge had been tailored to fit him, and this time, he was Captain Robusto Rotundo, captain of the pirate ship, SS Delaval. (He later became an engine driver.)

In 'Old Woman in a Shoe' we had noted a rabbit, Janet Grey, with a clear beautiful singing voice, so she was chosen to be 'Another Sleeping Beauty'. Thirty years on, married, with a teenage son, she still gives pleasure to local audiences.

Three stage-sets were required: a harbour road with the SS Delaval berthed alongside; the ship's deck-area; a desert isle with palm-trees bearing coconuts.

For the harbour scene, Mr Hardy painted a backcloth depicting cabins, bridge, funnel etc. In front of this, occupying the full breadth of the stage, was the hull and portside of the ship, built from hard-board suitably painted, with a real gangplank for boarding and disembarking.

For the deck-scene this arrangement was reversed, as the cast boarded from the back to take their places on deck which was the full stage with suitable deck-furnishings.

For the island-scene, only the coconuts required ingenuity; they had to be soft as the plot involved the monkey and school-children having a coconut-fight. We made dozens from the feet of old nylon stockings stuffed with rags and tissue paper, and stitched.

101

The brief fight was a highlight of the show with the younger children in the audience, as they fielded and threw back any coconuts which landed among them.

Mr Bennington gave considerable thought to the lighting effects and decided that the dance of the Bird of Glory, when everyone else lies curled up in a sleeping attitude, could be really spectacular.

At that time there was a celanese factory in Blyth from which we obtained several lengths of fluorescent material in bright colours. With it, the Needlework Club made plumage and wide-spreading wings for the bird. As night fell, and each dejected group found a sheltered spot on the isle to sleep, the lights were gradually dimmed until all were out and the stage in darkness. Then a hired black light was played on the stage as the Bird of Glory entered, spread its wings and began to dance to Rimsky-Korsakov's *Hindu Song*. The light picked out the glowing colours of the dancing bird; everything else was in darkness.

It was an effective scene and was the item selected to headline reports in local newspapers and in the *Daily Mail*. Its column 'Far and Near' devoted a couple of paragraphs to the show under the heading ''Black Magic' at the Panto', and began

> ''Members of New Delaval School Drama Club, Northumberland, are dabbling in 'Black Magic' in the interests of their forthcoming pantomime.''

The plot involved a poverty-stricken widow, Mrs Brannigan whose eight-year-old Barbara had heard a story at school about a hidden crock of gold. She wished she could find one so that her mother would not need to work so hard and wondered where it could be. Unwittingly, her mother said, 'Gold is always hidden on treasure islands, isn't it?'

Later Barbara was seen playing in Sam Hoyle's boat. Then she and the boat were missing, only the oars being found on the beach.

The play opens ten years later with Mrs Branningan talking to an old friend, saying she has never entirely given up hope that her daughter is alive.

The Demon King, accompanied by Little Demons and two Witches on broomsticks, gloats,

> I like to hear her grieve about her child so sweet and fair,
> I enjoy the thought of sadness in her heart;
> She little knows her daughter is now in my fond care
> On my precious 'Isle of Evil' in a distant foreign part.

On a sunny day, I whispered in her little shell-like ear,
And lured her with a tale of fairy gold,
A spell I placed upon her, when a lover doth appear
She will fall asleep and never wake to hear his love tale told.

Guarding and protecting her is a little native girl, Topsy, stolen by the Demons from an African kraal.

The Demon King can only exert his evil influence over people and 'torture them with grief and pain' if he knows their hearts' desire so the task of the Little Demons is to listen and spy until they discover everyone's secret wish.

The Fairy Queen, aided by Birds and Flowers, opposes the Demon King and tries to protect his victims.

Miss Antimacassar Freeze, a lean, angular school-marm, always exasperated and irritated by her class of mischievous schoolchildren, wishes she could find a husband.

Tinker Grumble, father of Midge and Spelk, is always taking things to pieces and not always putting them together again. His ambition is to dismantle a ship's engine.

His wife wishes for 'a bit of peace and quiet'.

His pal, George Jones, a pigeon-fancier, wishes he could try his prize bird over a really long distance.

Miss Constance Poorly wishes she could find a way to improve her health.

The Prince wishes to go on a long voyage before marrying any one of the pretty girls to whom his parents hopefully introduce him.

A means to apparently gratify their wishes is provided by Captain Robusto Rotundo, greedy and always hungry, supported by the big bullying mate, Roger Atom, the lugubrious cook, Noah Crackers, the cabin boy, Squib, the ship's monkey, Barmy, and a crew of sailors and sailor girls.

Captain and mate plan an educational cruise. After pocketing the passage money they intend to give the passengers one big rich meal which will make them so sea-sick and they will need nothing more until they are marooned on a desert isle.

All duly go aboard with their luggage:

Miss Freeze and the children.
Mrs Grumble and Tinker with his bag of tools.
George Jones with his pigeon.
Constance Poorly with her medicine chest and gramophone.
The Prince and his Page.

After a good dinner, everyone assembles on deck to spend the evening dancing and singing, mimicked by the monkey, until the ship begins to lurch, then slowly sink. A sailor appears shouting that the ship's engine has come adrift and knocked a hole in the bottom – Tinker had begun his dismantling. All take to the boats.

They are washed ashore, in separate groups, on the island where Barbara and Topsy have already lived for ten years.

Night falls. Each realizes his or her wish has come true, but it has not brought happiness. They gradually fall asleep as the Fairy Queen and Flowers appear followed by the Bird of Glory, which does a dance of hope and promise.

Next morning, the ship has beached and been made seaworthy again and all prepared to go aboard for the journey home, but Barbara has fallen asleep as the Prince declared his love, and they learn she is spellbound to sleep for fifty years. But Midge and Spelk say that their mother has always stated that their noise would waken the dead. They begin clapping, stamping, singing 'I've got a lovely bunch of coconuts,' and everyone else joins in until the din is terrific. Barbara awakes.

Captain Robusto Rotundo decides to marry Miss Freeze as she has proved so resourceful in providing food on the isle. He gives the ship to Roger Atom.

The final scene is the homecoming, Mrs Grant and Mrs Brannigan, the King and Queen, Mrs Jones with her husband's returned pigeon wait for the passengers to disembark from the SS Delaval.

The gang plank is lowered. Sailors and children form an aisle and Robusto Rotundo disembarks with his simpering bride, followed by all the other passengers. The curtain closes as the assembled cast sing, 'We'll go no more a-roving.'

The monkey, together with the mischievous children, were most popular with young members of the audience. The old fur coat had been adapted from dog-costume to monkey-outfit, aided by leather mitts, a brown balaclava, a monkey mask and a long tail. His stance and monkey-tricks improved at each performance until the middle of the show on the fourth evening, when my skirt was earnestly tugged as I stood in the wings with the script. I turned to face an agitated group of performers and a girl said, 'You'll have to come, miss. The monkey's taken his skin off and he's going home.'

I descended to the dressing-room to sort out the problem. Eating sweets and chewing gum were forbidden except during the interval; he had been reprimanded for eating sweets, allegedly containing gin, whilst the performance was in progress. He had resisted an attempt to confiscate them and was about to go home, taking his intoxicating sweets with him.

We reached a compromise: I would keep the sweets in my pocket and, at the interval, we would each eat one. Calm was restored and the show continued with the full ship's complement.

That monkey, Frank Jackson, became a painter and decorator and later a manager on a building site.

20.

No sooner was 'Another Sleeping Beauty' over and school-life restored to normal, than evening rehearsals with the Old Scholars' Drama Club had to be intensified, as Blyth Miners' Welfare Hall was booked for 26th, 27th and 28th March and tickets for 'Cinderella' were on sale.

My husband and I seemed to spend almost as much time at school as at home: he had kindly made himself responsible for the construction of the scenery, and every member of Staff became voluntarily involved.

Some evenings, principals came to our home so that we could rehearse in greater comfort. After the rehearsal they would sit beside the fire, having coffee and biscuits, and gossiping. Then they would wash the cups and saucers and go home.

One Ugly Sister, Tapioca, was always reluctant to leave and had to be urged on by the others. One evening as she stood up to go, she said, 'It's peaceful here. *You* don't know what life is, Mrs Wrigley.'

I found out what she meant the week before the show.

I arrived on that particular evening to a quiet classroom: no records, no laughter, just a subdued group. Tapioca had withdrawn from the pantomime; she was not coming to the Drama Club anymore. There had been a family row, and her ballgown thrown on the fire. She had put so much work into it; it had been voluminous and striking, made from many scraps of material.

I decided to go to her home and see what could be done.

The door was opened by her mother, who at once shouted upstairs. 'Here's the teacher, Mary. I telt you she would come.'

I was invited into a room of some disarray whilst her mother went upstairs to urge or coax Mary down. On a sofa, boy twins, aged about six, were playing with Snap cards, but instead of saying 'Snap!' when identical cards appeared, they shouted, 'They're mine, ye bugger.'

Eventually, Mary came down and back to school with me. With help from the other girls, she was to make another gown for the ball and I would look after it for her until it was required. Her normal high spirits were soon restored and rehearsal went ahead.

Except for a boy who elected to be Stage Manager and a girl who was Volunteer Music Librarian, each one of the thirty-five club members had a speaking part, however brief. There was plenty of scope for song and dance; swift-moving dialogue and clowning kept the pace up.

The humorous side of the show was mainly provided by Baron and Baroness Pepper and their two ugly daughters, Tapioca and Semolina, but they were bolstered by the Broker's Men, their neighbours' children (one too fat and one too thin) and Blossom McFactor, a beauty specialist, Gertie Gavotte, a dancing teacher, and Ella Cushon an authority on etiquette, who came to prepare the Ugly Sisters for the ball.

To give individual performers opportunity without incongruity, a talent competition was an integral part of the Royal Ball with a prize of £100 for the winner. This enabled Baron Pepper to play his drums (and pay his debts) and the Ugly Sisters to do their hilarious Shotgun Boogie dance.

Cinderella was suitably sweet-natured and sang her plaintive song well, cherished and supported by a faithful Buttons. Her song, 'Sitting By the Fire and Dreaming' was composed by Mr Pollard and Miss Hargreaves.

Not only had everyone rehearsed well, they had sold tickets assiduously and full houses were assured.

The *Blyth News* report begins

"Many people who had "gone on chance" had to be turned away from the final performance of Cinderella presented by New Delaval Old Scholars' Drama Club at Blyth Miners' Welfare Hall, where there was a capacity audience."

Actually, it was not quite the final performance, because we revived Cinderella for one evening the following December in order to entertain the patients at Stannington Children's Sanatorium.

I shall never forget the faces of the bedridden children as the complete cast moved from bed to bed, dancing and singing in the wards, talking to the patients, Cinderella in silver and white with her smart long-legged Prince in plumed hat; the Ugly Sisters in their outrageous ballgowns, Baron Pepper and his nagging Baroness; Fairy Queen and Demon etc.

Some lonely children found new friends that evening whom they would see again.

One little girl, four years old, had never had a visitor of her own during two years there; her parents had gone to live in the south of England and given up all contact. Santa Claus visited her that year.

It was a moving and worthwhile occasion for us all.

I have been looking at the 'Cinderella' programme and remembering each 'old scholar', some of whom I still meet as friends. 'Man with a Dog', now a fireman, was here last Saturday.

Baroness Pepper emigrated to Canada. After reading in a *Blyth News*, sent by her mother, of our retirement, she wrote to my husband and me. I quote from her letter

"I often cast my mind back to those far-off days, and, oh, what happy days they were, when we used to be in the pantomimes. I want to thank you, even though it is so long ago, for giving me lovely memories. To this day you are fondly remembered."

A year later, whilst on holiday in England, she called to see us, accompanied by her husband and fourteen-year-old son. She still works for the Investment Dealers' Association of Canada on the educational side.

Blossom McFactor, who became a Queen Alexandra nursing-sister, also lives in Canada, with her husband and three daughters, and keeps in touch with me.

Baron Pepper became a joiner and later, north-eastern technical adviser for a well-known kitchen-equipment firm. He also maintained a friendship with us; we have had a Christmas card from him each year for at least thirty years.

I have photographs of Semolina's wedding, but that was a long time ago. She lives in Scotland and has, I think, six children, now grown-up.

Tapioca never married, but has a son and grandchild and has never lost her invincible high spirits.

This year, 1952, had begun with these two popular drama productions and succeeding events seem to indicate a healthy school year.

At the Annual Sports Meeting in May, Delaval girls' team won the Blyth Schools' Athletics Association Trophy, competing against six other schools, all with more pupils. They had been coached mainly during lunch breaks and after school by Messrs Wrigley, Bennington and Pollard. I just presented them 'on the day'.

A boy, who now has a painting and decorating business of his own, painted a ten feet by four feet mural inside the school depicting the Houses.

One rainy mid-morning break, Mr Pollard found a tall, well-built top form boy sitting writing, apparently putting his thoughts down on paper. His thoughts were printed in the *Ashington Advertiser* that May.

> *To be a Man*
> You are not a man when you have grown;
> You are not a man when you are big and strong;
> You are not a man when you are bigger than all others,
> And, if you think you are, you're wrong.
> When all men beneath your blows are weakened,
> That's when you'll trip and stumble forward;
> And that's when they will take advantage;
> And that's when you become a coward.
>
> But if men live at peace beside you,
> And if you help them when you can,
> If men are sad when they're without you,
> That's when you become a man.
>
> Charles Davis.

On a beautiful July day, financed by pantomime proceeds, the whole school, and a few Old Scholars set out by bus at nine o'clock for Bamburgh. There, we visited the Castle, the Church in whose grounds Grace Darling is buried, and the little Grace Darling museum where a lock of her hair and her nightcap seemed to attract more interest than the boat in which she rowed out to the shipwrecked *Forfar*.

Yet below the activity, there was a current of unease, which reached its peak in July.

Newlands, the first comprehensive school in Blyth, was to open in September, so boundary lines had been altered to enable as many children as possible to gain the advantage of its modern facilities. That meant our numbers would be reduced by about a quarter.

We realized some change was inevitable but we regretted, indeed resented, that youngsters in their final year were to be included.

Mr Soulsby announced the forthcoming changes on Speech Day, saying he had come to 'the unhappy side' of his report, adding, 'A school is a family and when you interfere with families you cause pain. I would be a coward if I did not make a protest even though the new school has tremendous facilities which are lacking at Delaval.'

Parents wrote letters of protest to the *Newcastle Journal* and *Blyth News*, and complained to the Education Committee. A few wrote to the Ministry of Education.

Interviewed by the press, an official at the local Education Office said that the children should understand that the move was for their own benefit.

'They are getting an opportunity their predecessors never had.' He added that, because of the new situation, 'tuition would improve.'

Parents of top class children made a special appeal to Mr Soulsby to see if he could do something about it, so he requested and was granted, an interview with the Director of Education for Northumberland. He asked me to accompany him and we went together to County Hall on the appointed Saturday morning.

I sat in a corridor waiting until the interview was over. I could see by his face as he came out that he had been unsuccessful. He said, 'I should like to sit down quietly somewhere.' He led the way to the dilapidated Church of All Saints nearby and we sat quietly in a pew for a while. Then he stood up, smiled, said, 'Never despair!' and we set off for home.

We always tried to plan activities involving the whole school on the last day of the summer term to leave as little opportunity for grief as possible, but there were always weeping girls in corners. Boys tended to follow one around, the occasional one with an armful of English books, assuring me he would keep them for ever.

This term ending was more dismal than usual, with tears all round.

It was especially sad for the Staff, for we had been a happy band of workers and, because of the reorganization Mr Butterworth, Mr Crossland, Mr Hardy and Miss Horn had to go too.

Mr Hardy went to be full time Art Master at Newlands which was to become noted for the high quality of its Art. When he bade us goodbye he said he hoped I would always call on him to help with scenery when panto time came round.

The seven parents who had protested to the Ministry of Education eventually won their appeal; consequently, five senior girls and two boys returned to Delaval the following January and two more after Easter.

I have a newspaper cutting depicting five girls returning with arms linked and broad smiles. I met one of them, the champion hurdler, Betty Lawson, whilst walking in Humford Woods recently and was introduced to her children.

21.

Despite depleted numbers, both of Staff and pupils, Mr Soulsby was resolved that the quality of school-life should be unimpaired and the needs of each individual met.

The remaining Staff had the ability and will to continue specialist teaching in all the subjects required but considerable organization was needed to fit them into the bounds of a timetable. A working schedule was attained after juggling with times, names and subjects: it was rather like doing a complicated jig-saw.

As pupils reached school-leaving age, we were still able to direct those who could benefit from it to places of further education; Ashington Technical College; a secretarial college; the College of Industrial Design; Polytechnic; a catering college. A few were prepared for the Civil Service Examination.

'Follow-up' showed that the standard of education reached before they left us enabled students to fit without difficulty into new places of learning and to be successful in formal technical and academic examinations, including GCE. At least two reached Universities and gained BSc degrees.

The clubs, including The Old Scholars, continued to flourish and we were able to accept a greater percentage of the school complement into the Drama Club by keeping the number the same.

At the end of February 1953, our version of Red Riding Hood was staged.

The traditional story was maintained, but it was set against her environment, the village where she lived with her mother and her younger sister Farthing, who always wore a blue hood, and villagers such as the lazy Egbert Patch, his nagging wife Petunia, and their two mischievous sons, Mrs Twirp and her twin daughters and other children.

In the wood nearby was a gipsy encampment with a matriarchal Old Crone, her brutal son, Lasher and Serena, a pretty girl whom they had kidnapped in a previous place as she talked to birds and sang, and a band of gipsy girls, gipsy men and mischievous gipsy children.

Red Riding Hood's grandmother lived in a cottage beyond the wood and a friendly woodcutter lived nearby.

The wood was also the dwelling place of the Witch with her band of servile Demons and pet wolf, Slinker, and of the Queen of the Wood and her Nymphs.

A Prince with his attendant lords and their ladies frequented the wood to enjoy the gipsy songs and dances. He was especially attracted by Serena's singing.

The Witch hates everyone except the Wolf which she adores.

> "I only love one creature
> On this earth;
> My pet, my sharp-fanged wolf,
> Who, howling, prowls
> And kills at my behest
> Milk-hearted victims."

The Wolf particularly wants

> ".....a girl
> Who lives near the wood;
> She must taste tender
> For she's always good;
> She wears a red cape
> And a little red hood,
> Very dainty garments
> To wrap my food."

Intermingled circumstances enable the Prince to marry Serena, the gipsies to tell fortunes, pilfer, sell pegs and brooms, and dance and sing, as the traditional Red Riding Hood story is worked out. The finale is the campfire in the woods to celebrate the weddings of the Prince and Serena and the gipsies, Lasher and Hotcha, with everyone taking part in the merriment.

Serena, Sleeping Beauty of the previous show, was now more mature and assured, her voice stronger, still sweet and expressive.

The show was relatively easy to costume as much could be improvised from normal everyday wear. In our changed circumstances, Domestic Science and

Needlework were linked, so Mrs Mowatt had taken over the Needlework Club and worked diligently with the girls. They turned out batches of embroidered gipsies' waistcoats, black cat-suits with close fitting black hoods attached for Demons and diaphanous floating pale green draperies for Queen of the Wood and her Nymphs.

By adding a big wolf head, made out of paper mache and painted, and an appropriate tail, the fur coat became a wolf-suit.

There were three stage-sets; the village street; a woodland scene; the interior of the grandmother's cottage. Most of the scenery was adapted from props stored after previous pantomimes, but two caravans were constructed, one showing the open door at the back with steps leading up to it on which the Old Crone sat.

It was a bright colourful show, cast and audience enjoying the rhythm and vigour of the gipsy music. Mr Pollard and Miss Hargreaves again provided original numbers, two of which were especially popular. 'I wish I had a man,' sung by Hotcha, the gipsy comedienne, and 'A happy little whistling song', which the Prince taught the village children to sing and whistle so that they would not be afraid in the depths of the wood. It was much whistled in the school precincts over succeeding weeks.

The Witch, surrounded by leering Demons and flanked by the Wolf, was suitably malevolent and menacing. 'She' was a 'He'. A boy had auditioned for this role and played it very well. At the close of the final performance, he told me he hoped to be on the next pantomime, but did not want to be a witch because rounding-up little Demons and keeping them under control (on and off-stage) was too exhausting.

Extract from one press cutting

> "A witty script, well-interpreted by those who acted in it, and considerably enlivened by a troupe of gipsy dancing-girls and contrasting Nymph and Demon dances."

In May, came the last show to be given by the Old Scholars.

Youth Clubs, run by specially trained young professional leaders were coming into being nationally and one would later be inaugurated at New Delaval. A majority of the Old Scholars were in the eighteen to twenty-one years age-range; a few were contemplating marriage; a few due to enter National Service in the Army, Navy or RAF. The younger ones became the nucleus of the Youth Club and we transferred our funds to it. But first, we presented 'The Magic Carpet', which ran to capacity audiences for five nights.

The script contained quick repartee, but it relied heavily on local atmosphere and allusions. The plot was zany, yet, somehow, it was fun. It was played with an exhilaration which gave it an apparent realism. Its success was due to comic contrasts, singing and dancing, but above all, to local flavour.

There were six smart girls in the club who were good dancers in a pseudo-ballet, movement-to-music kind of way, one girl in particular being able to improvise with grace and imagination to classical music. So there were to be three 'principal girls' and three 'principal boys'.

After a shipwreck, three little girls on a raft had been washed ashore in 'Araby' and reared at the court of the Sultan, Plaza Roxy d'Essoldo.

When they grow up, it becomes their task to keep the Sultan amused, Starella by dancing, Elnora by singing and Dagmar by telling stories.

All goes well until a British sailing-ship anchors nearby and the girls fall in love with its three illustrious passengers, Prince Rafael and Dukes Simon and Leo. Permission to return to England with them is refused and any unauthorised attempt to leave will result in death for all at the knife-point of Alley-Barber, the royal executioner.

The Evil Genie surfaces to keep strife stirring, but the Good Genie departs on his Magic Carpet to seek help for the victims. He lands at Delaval on Gala Day and offers free lottery tickets, with the carpet as the prize. It is won by a miner, Jonner, who, prompted by the Genie's influence, organizes a Magic Carpet trip.

On to the carpet dance the Coconut-shy man, the Housey-Housey caller, the Fortune teller, Professor Archie Ology, Mrs Flutter and her daughter Dizzy, Jonner and his friend Titch with their respective wives Aspirin and Kodene, and daughters Aspidistra and Gorgonzola. They shout the magic words, 'Gee Whizz' and away the Carpet flies.

The rest of the show deals with the hullabaloo caused by the Carpet's return to Araby. All works to a satisfactory denouement, of course, the only frustrated person being Alley-Barber with his constantly-whetted knives unused. The prisoners are allowed to go free, because the Sultan has found other ways to relieve the tedium of his days. Aspidistra and Gorgonzola teach him a new language, 'Geordie', which he soon masters, with amusing consequences. They do wild dances and sing to his drumming.

Aspirin and Kodene, the two wives, emancipate the Sultana.

Only two sets were needed, the Gala field with stalls and tent, and the Sultan's courtyard, suitably oriental.

The girls made or contrived the costuming, with some Staff assistance.

The three principal boys wore tights, short embroidered velvet tunics and plumed hats, the girls long diaphanous dresses. The harem girls wore gauzy turquoise trousers drawn in at the ankle and short black boleros with long turquoise sleeves, their mid-riffs were bare.

A couple of weeks before the show the young man to have been Professor Archie Ology had to leave to work elsewhere, so his place was taken by Mr Pollard, much to the delight of the cast and the local audience.

The *Newcastle Journal* report paid tribute to the acting ability of 'local factory workers, shop-girls and apprentices', adding, 'Originality is always the keynote of New Delaval productions and this is no exception.'

The Sultan, Ivan with his drums, had been the Baron in Cinderella, the Sultana, the Baroness, Aspidistra and Gorgonzola, the Ugly Sisters. Newcomer as comedian was Alley-Barber who had been Accumulator in the school production, 'Old Woman in the Shoe'. When he reached manhood his natural cheerfulness and wit persisted. It was a shock to us all when he was killed in a road accident.

22.

The year, 1953, was one of outstanding national significance, highlighted by the Conquest of Everest and the Coronation of Queen Elizabeth II.

From the day the climb began, the pupils followed on maps the progress of the mountaineers, and some made scrapbooks of the expedition from newspaper cuttings.

Prior to a three-day holiday to celebrate the Coronation, on May 29th, the school assembled in the Delaval Miners' Welfare Hall to hear a talk given by a Methodist minister, the Rev F Wilson, on the spiritual significance of the Coronation and to receive souvenir copies of *Northumberland*, embossed with the school badge.

At the inter-school Athletics Meeting, New Delaval gained second place over-all, Blyth Grammar School achieving first place and the new comprehensive school, Newlands third. Yet we had fewer than 200 pupils on the school roll.

The school trip, which had a historical slant, was to Corbridge, Hexham and the Roman Wall.

In his Speech Day report, Mr Soulsby quoted the Duke of Edinburgh's statement that 'the most important factors about a school are, firstly, the teachers, secondly, the pupils, and thirdly, the building.'

The prizes were presented by the Rev George Chadwick, Vicar of St Bede's, a man of deep spirituality and humanity, well-known locally for his philanthropy to anyone in need. He said that friendliness was a special characteristic of New Delaval School and that every aspect of school-life was a part of one great aim – preparation for the wider world the pupils must face in the future.

The closing months of the year were marked by sadness. Mr Soulsby's health had been deteriorating for sometime and on October 16th he entered hospital with a very low blood-count (but with undiminished spirit). It was

December 16th before he returned to school and, even then, was not fully recovered, but he wished to be there for the presentation of leaving-gifts to JAN Pollard, who had been promoted to the Headship of a country school.

JAN's contribution to the welfare of the school had been outstanding and we knew that we should miss him as a teacher, and a friend.

Shortly before the school closed for the Christmas holiday, senior pupils were taken to Morpeth one evening to hear Peter Scott lecture on his visit to Tierra del Fuego. He received members of the Scott Fellowship afterwards and autographed copies of *The Great White South*.

Diverse circumstances affected the pattern of school-life in 1954.

A permanent teacher to replace Mr Pollard was not appointed until March when Mr Jeffrey Crozier joined the Staff.

Mr Soulsby was frail; absent from school for occasional days, unable to work with his customary vigour when there. So I had extra classes to supervise and additional administrative chores: we had never had a school clerk.

My mother was seriously ill at home and I wished to spend as much time with her as possible, so I did very little voluntary extraneous work, which meant no pantomime.

Boys and girls, however, participated in all inter-school sporting activities, and academically, the school maintained its normal momentum. One girl and two boys recommended for the 13+ examination were successful and they transferred (with some reluctance on their part) to Blyth Grammar School after the summer holiday.

Three boys received RSPCA awards for rescuing a cat from the top of a telegraph pole opposite the school, completing the operation just before the Fire Brigade arrived to do it.

My mother died early in July.

In September, the Drama Club began rehearsals of 'The Lost Totem' for presentation early the following year.

Then, in October, we were informed that the school was to have a General Inspection on November 3rd, 4th and 5th. Three of Her Majesty's Inspectors would be there throughout and additional ones part of the time, after which a report would be published.

However conscientiously and successfully a school is run such news rouses a feeling of apprehension. Indeed, I think it might be better if a team of HMI's arrived unannounced. In some schools great preparations ensue: ambitious projects are begun and classroom displays arranged. I even know of one school where the gardening teacher borrowed pot-plants from a local park.

None of this occurred at Delaval, where every classroom always had a show of plants supplied by the gardening classes. The boys reared plants from cuttings in a sunny corner of the woodwork room.

Mr Soulsby merely asked everyone to be punctual, to work as usual, and to see all exercise books were checked up-to-date. Nevertheless, we all had this feeling of apprehensive expectancy.

In the event, the visit was interesting and exhilarating, all inspectors apparently satisfied with the general atmosphere and attainment. The leader spent much time with the English classes and took bundles of exercise books away to peruse. When he returned them, he complimented the pupils on the standard and appearance of their work. Two 'My Magazine' notebooks, he asked if he might retain to display elsewhere. The two girls to whom they belonged, whilst conscious of the honour, rather regretted the loss of their original work.

After school on the final day of the inspection, the HMI's met the school Governors and made certain recommendations about the fabric of the building. Sometime later the official report arrived:-

MINISTRY OF EDUCATION

REPORT BY H.M. INSPECTORS ON
New Delaval County Secondary School,
Blyth, Northumberland.
INSPECTED ON 3rd, 4th and 5th NOVEMBER, 1954.
Premises.

The premises were built as a colliery school in the 1860s and are at present rented from The National Coal Board. The School originally served the mining village of New Delaval, which has since largely disappeared, leaving the School somewhat isolated, approached only by rutted roads and surrounded by pit spoil and wasteland. Accommodation provided by the main building consists of seven classrooms, two small staff-rooms and sanitary offices. Four corridors, meeting in the form of a cross, act as cloakrooms and place of assembly; the end walls of two corridors are fitted with wash-basins and a section of one corridor has been curtained off to provide a changing room for the girls. A wooden hut, erected on part of the School garden in 1936, provides three rooms for Housecraft, Science and Woodwork. Recent improvements to the premises include the laying of a paved playground and the installation of electric light and two new boilers. The midday meal, transported from a central kitchen, is served in the Miners' Welfare Hall near the School and is taken by some 30% of the pupils. A piece of rough land some 200 yards from the School is used for games, but this land is used also for other local activities, including fairs and circuses, and may therefore not be regarded as a satisfactory school playing field. It is understood that the tennis courts on the Miners' Welfare Field were once frequently used by the School, but this is unfortunately no longer so.

The School is in urgent need of interior redecoration; the provision of good pictures and curtains in the corridors would do much to lessen the stark austerity of the interior; the wooden ramp at the only entrance to the main building and the difference in levels in the first stretch of corridor are potentially dangerous. The floors in at least two classrooms are in need of repair. The lack of a School Hall for dancing, dramatic work and indoor physical activities is a serious handicap; it is suggested that, if available, the Miners' Welfare Hall would provide a good substitute.

Furniture and Equipment.
The School is furnished with old dual desks. Many of them have worn badly, the seats have a pronounced slope, and pupils may no longer hold a good sitting posture on them. In addition to this, very few desks are large enough for the older pupils. The work benches in the Science, Housecraft and Needlecraft rooms are all in need of repair.

In general the School is well equipped with books, tools and mechanical aids; the School's own stock of books and periodicals together with the loan-collection from the Public Library merit the proper care and display possible in a Library; a partly used room in the main building might well be adapted for this purpose. A corner of the Woodwork room is at present used for certain Gardening experiments and indoor culture; this work is already good and its value would be greatly enhanced by the provision of a greenhouse.

Organisation and Standards of Work.
The necessary revision of catchment areas following the opening of the Newlands County Secondary School in 1952 reduced the roll at this School by roughly a quarter. The present number on the books is 176 arranged in six Forms; the less able pupils in the first and second years together make up Form 2 and those in the third and fourth years make up Form 4. In the circumstances this is realistic and appropriate organisation and the School has done well in ensuring that its life and work have been in no way disrupted by the inevitable difficulties of organisation. The Head Master, who came to the School in 1944,

has with him a staff of seven qualified teachers; together they make up a well balanced and competent team with, in general, a teaching ability above the average; their work is marked by a very high degree of loyalty and devotion to the School and its traditions.

In order to overcome some of the difficulties caused by the premises the time-table is arranged to give lesson periods after 11 o'clock of at least one hour. It was evident during the Inspection that this is not a satisfactory arrangement in a number of subjects. The allotment of time to some subjects also needs to be revised.

The schemes of work in all subjects have been thoughtfully planned and prepared. After two years operation some of them now show the need for revision particularly with a view to suiting the work more to the pupils' needs and abilities. The teaching throughout the School is specialist; the loss of pupils and Staff in 1952 necessitated an allocation of some subjects to teachers who were not necessarily qualified in those subjects; these changes were obviously accepted willingly in the best interests of the School, for there is no sign of neglect or indifferent work in any subject of the curriculum.

A proper pride in the appearance and finish of work is encouraged throughout the School; the example set by the specimen work of some of the teachers and the exercises in Bookcraft contribute noticeably to this. The practical subjects for boys, Woodwork and Gardening, are well taught and by a well planned progression the boys are led to work which calls for a good standard of skill and exercise of initiative and imagination. The fourth year in particular are encouraged to work to their own designs. Housecraft and Needlecraft, although perhaps not correctly balanced as regards time allotted also make full demands on the pupils and are producing fully satisfactory results. These four subjects are taught by two teachers who give reality to the work by constantly showing the practical everyday significance of it. This is true also of the work in Science, which is given even greater educational value by its frequent reference to other subjects of the curriculum. The work in Mathematics, which is shared by two Masters, reaches a good standard in Arithmetic and includes some algebra and geometry for the more able pupils. The various techniques included in the Art and Crafts course are carefully and methodically taught; the range of activities could profitably be widened, and improved storage and display facilities are very necessary. The lack of facilities for Physical Education greatly reduces the range of possible activities. In the circumstances, and until suitable indoor accommodation becomes available, it would be advisable to concentrate on work which does not need elaborate equipment or apparatus. The further development of skill at games, athletics, and various forms of dancing are possibilities. The morning assembly and small services held on other occasions make a definite contribution to the spiritual life of the School. Religious Instruction, taken entirely by the Head Master, consists largely of a sincere study of the Bible. This subject however needs more time than is at present given to it. Music, consisting of choral singing and certain School broadcasts, is obviously enjoyed by the whole School. Teachers, and on occasion the pupils themselves, compose words and music for school concerts and plays. The prescribed length of periods for Music tends to be too long, although the work is fully appropriate and calls up willing response even from the older boys who are having difficulty with their voices. The teaching of English is shared by the Senior Mistress and a young Master who joined the staff this year. The syllabuses, devised by the Senior Mistress, provide an unusually wide variety of work ranging from the consolidation of reading skill to the writing of original poems and plays. some of this latter work shows, by its freshness and technical skill, that the imagination of the syllabus is being matched by very good teaching. The influence of this teaching is apparent in all subjects. With only one or two exceptions lesson notes or summaries are, from the first year onwards, the work of the pupils themselves.

Conclusion

Within the field of possibilities open to it the School is providing a sound Secondary Education both in book studies and in the normal practical subjects. All pupils are given work appropriate to them and an individual rate of progress is encouraged. Evidence of this is seen in the fact that at the end of last term ten pupils moved on from this School to other and more advanced forms of education. The Head Master and the staff of teachers show in all their work that they have the interests of their pupils at heart. Assured of this concern, the children respond willingly to all demands made upon them; visitors to the School cannot fail to be impressed by the warmth and friendliness of the School community, in which every individual is encouraged to feel of some importance and consequence. The present strength of the Old Scholars' Association gives proof of the deep and lasting value which the School has upon their lives.

APPENDIX.

NUMBERS AND AGES OF PUPILS IN FORMS

Number of Pupils in the School on 5.11.54 whose ages were:

Form	Total No. of Pupils	Average Age Y M			11 and under 12	12 and under 13	13 and under 14	14 and under 15	15 and under 16
1	39	11	9	B	16	3	—	—	—
				G	17	3	—	—	—
2	26	12	0	B	6	9	1	—	—
				G	8	2	—	—	—
3	39	12	8	B	—	17	3	—	—
				G	—	4	5	—	—
4	26	13	8	B	—	—	11	4	—
				G	—	1	8	1	1
5	26	13	9	B	—	—	9	4	—
				G	—	—	9	4	—
6	30	14	8	B	—	—	—	15	3
				G	—	—	—	12	—
Totals	176	—		B	22	29	24	23	3
				G	25	10	22	17	1

The Inspectors' report gladdened us all, especially as the success of Mr Soulsby's aims, his unobtrusive leadership and his devotion to the school had been officially recognised. This boost to his morale was to sustain him in his increasing struggle against ill health.

However, he was able to attend school regularly for the first three months of 1955, and contributed his usual encouragement and enthusiasm to preparations for 'The Last Totem'.

It had a Cowboy v Indian theme, but the basic message was a concept of world peace: the idea that people of all races can live peacefully in the same environment, given goodwill and mutual understanding. Evil in the world was represented by a band of coyotes whose sole aim was to stir up strife. They set fire to a covered wagon, driven by a man accompanied by his baby girl. The man was burnt to death, but the child was rescued by a tribe of Indians who took her with them and named her Solawee, meaning Little Lost One.

The coyotes stole the Totem of the Indians and hid it in cowboy territory. When the braves have no hunting success and food is scarce, the tribe blamed their ill-luck on the loss of the Totem and the presence of Solawee.

The Cowboys are short of drinking-water as their spring of clear water has dried up in the drought, only a muddy yellow stream remaining which is used for washing. They cannot bring water from the hills because of the Indian hostility.

One evening they are reduced to a half cup of coffee each at the evening meal. They retire for the night, anxious and thirsty, leaving the horse Tigger, belonging to the children, tethered outside.

When all is still, the coyotes come in, searching for scraps of food and steal the horse. The mischievous children, Twink, Wobbly and Boy Dodger come to raid the larder, find the horse gone and set out in search of it.

The coyotes loose the horse into the camp of the Indians who welcome it as a gift of food in answer to their prayers. Omasta, the chief, orders it to be tethered to a tree, ready for sacrifice next morning and leaves two squaws, Gabagobba and Insomnia to guard it through the night. Gabagobba talks herself to sleep.

The children creep in, lasso and gag Insomnia and tie her to the tree, untether the horse and ride away on it. They have noted with astonishment a White Indian among the sleepers.

Next morning the Indians are furious at the disappearance of their breakfast, blame it superstitiously on the white child and decide she must be sacrificed if they cannot find the horse.

Back at the ranch, the children's story of a white Indian is believed only by Aunt Sula and she slips away with them to the Indian camp, where all four are grabbed and tied, as Solawee already is, to trees. Omasta gives orders for a funeral pyre to be built for Solawee.

As the Indians move about the stage collecting branches, Merryhaha, a girl Indian who loves Solawee, surreptitiously loosens Boy Dodger and bids him fetch help.

As the Indian girls dance with increasing menace, to de Falla's 'Ritual Fire Dance', round the pyre where Solawee is tied, the braves hold 'flaring brands' ready to throw to ignite the fire. Just as the climax is reached the ranchers arrive. Mabin and Omasta prevent their people from fighting until they have discussed the situation. The Indians agree to free the four children in exchange for Tigger the horse. Tigger is tied again to a tree, now to be sacrificed at sunset unless the lost Totem is found.

Back at the ranch house the women go in sadly to pack all the household goods whilst the men round up the cattle for the trail to a new place. The children sit disconsolately outside. To try to forget about Tigger's fate, they decide to race twigs in the Yellow Burn. Soon they are in it too, squelching their feet down deep into the mud until Wobbly's foot is cut by something sharp. They search for the offending object and drag out the lost Totem.

Merryhaha comes looking for Solawee, sees the Totem and kneels down. Solawee bids her fetch Omasta and save the horse.

Peaceful relationship ensues. The Indians free their springs to the ranchers; they give the Indians meat. Tigger is returned to his owners.

At sunset all come together at the Indian location to celebrate, agreeing to live side by side and share resources thenceforth.

After Tigger has danced to 'A Four-legged Friend', everyone sings, 'Smoking the pipe of peace' as ceremonial pipes are passed around and sunset fades.

The play gave us scope for square-dancing and traditional cowboys songs such as 'Poor Lonesome Cowboy' and 'The Cowboy's Prayer'.

There was a great construction of bows and arrows, pipes of peace and flaming torches. Sacks of twigs and branches were gathered for the pyre. The beach was combed for suitable birds' feathers which Miss Laws, combined Domestic Science and Needlework teacher, dyed, and these were used to make Indian head-dresses.

Only two scenes were needed, the exterior of the ranch-house and the Indian location.

Whatever shortcomings Delaval might suffer, its good fortune with staffing continued. Mr Pollard had seemed irreplaceable, yet Mr Crozier fitted perfectly into his place, entering wholeheartedly into all aspects of school-life. He did not compose music, but he could design scenery, and find simple ways to improvise what could have been complicated sets. He also did the speciality make-up with expertise.

The woodworkers built a ranch-house, with a trestle table and forms outside.

Mr Crozier designed a stage-set about a foot high and fairly long. Set obliquely at one side of the stage it looked like reeds fringing a stream and this was the Yellow Burn. Behind it the Totem could be laid flat, out of sight of the audience.

He designed the Totem, too, a fearsome creature with six legs and a big head which could be hooked on, and unhooked from, a tall post at the Indian location.

The show had a new venue. Because we had no school hall the Education Authority recommended that we use the hall at Newlands School, subject to the Headmaster's approval.

I asked Mr Soulsby if he would write to the Headmaster, Mr Davies, and he said, 'We'll go and see him'.

We went one afternoon, were cordially received and given cups of tea. Mr Soulsby and Mr Davies were both great talkers and at once engaged in a long and animated conversation whilst I sat and listened. Then Mr Soulsby stood up to come away and Mr Davies bade us goodbye. I tried to politely intervene without success.

When we were driving away, I said, 'You forgot to ask if we could use the hall'.

'So I did,' Mr Soulsby said, laughing. 'Never mind, you ring him up in the morning.' Which I did, and suitable dates were arranged, including two rehearsal afternoons.

It was a comparatively big stage with ample standing space at the sides and plenty of rostra for building different levels, excellent for mountain background at the Indian location.

The lighting was a delight to Mr Bennington who was able to make the sacrifice of Solawee scene really dramatic and the peaceful eventide-ending beautiful.

The horse was the highlight for children who saw the show. The skin was given us by someone at Newsham where it had been used at a gala-day and a new head was fashioned at school. Once the two boys had mastered the art of synchronising their movements, they had great fun. It danced, kicked, stampeded, pursued, and sulked with crossed legs.

When Mr Hardy, by then Art Master at Newlands, saw our stage equipment he said he felt really sorry that we obviously needed his help no longer. However, he brought some paints and gave our horse a piebald look 'for old-times sake'.

The show appealed as a spectacle: the checked shirts and bright swinging skirts of the ranchgirls; the black-suited coyotes with leering green faces cavorting in green and blue spot-lights; the Totem; Indian feathers, beads and braiding.

Half a page of photographs appeared in the *Newcastle Evening Chronicle*; ranchers at their evening meal; Omasta in his magnificent head-dress; Tigger with Boy Dodger; the full cast – 75 in all.

Extract from the *Blyth News*.

"Indians, cowboys, ranch-girls and coyotes blazed a trail across the Newlands County Secondary School stage in an original play staged by New Delaval County Secondary School. The action gave plenty of scope for colourful scenes, interspersed by Indian lyrics and rousing hill-billy choruses."

Incidentally Bob Dodger (Ronnie Barker) later became Headmaster of a comprehensive school in Lancashire.

An innovation was a first night which was semi-rehearsal; free to the local Over-Sixty Club and with very cheap tickets for children under eleven years of age. This type of 'first night' became customary because it proved beneficial all-round: cheap entertainment for the elderly and very young and a good test for the cast who had to carry on valiantly despite the restlessness and noise in the auditorium. When anything serious or romantic was in progress, the youngsters ate their crackling crisps, sucked at bottles of mineral water and went out and in to the lavatories. They booed the 'baddies' and cheered the horse, 'shushed' loudly by the old people. A few of the latter were usually hard-of-hearing and they tended to carry on conversations in audible voices during the action. Repartee often went unnoticed, so the laughter which spurs players on was missing.

After such trials, performers were able to face the responsive audiences of ensuing evenings with lively confidence.

An HMI who came to see 'The Lost Totem' said he often found school drama producers erred by choosing plays which were either over-ambitious or puerile, and suggested I submit my scripts to a publisher.

I tried 'The Lost Totem' as its theme was topical and it was not localised. It was returned with a letter in which the dialogue and plot were commended, but it was turned down as being too difficult for schools to stage and as having too large a cast.

The financial proceeds of the show enhanced the School Fund and paid for the Annual School Excursion. This took place in July, when the whole school, accompanied, at his own request, by an *Evening Chronicle* photographer, visited Alnwick, Bamburgh and Seahouses.

At Seahouses, everyone admired the new lifeboat, named *Grace Darling* and, afterwards, the captain of Grace Darling House presented a donation on behalf of the school to the Chairman of the Lifeboat Guild.

Mr Soulsby wanted his pupils to be aware of their own county and proud of their heritage. Besides excursions around Northumberland, he regularly showed the assembled school selections from his large collection of colour slides and talked about the historical and geographical background; the flora and fauna. He outlined the development of their own town from saltpans and sailing ships to coal-mines and cargo-ship construction.

They were proud of their heritage and of their school. This was evinced when the school narrowly escaped being burnt-down. One Monday evening a

129

past scholar was walking past the school when he noticed a bright glare at one window. He ran to the caretaker's house and he and the caretaker entered the school to find a six-foot flame gushing from a lead gas pipe not far from the main gas meter. The caretaker turned off the gas and discovered six inches of piping had melted. Woodwork and walls nearby were badly scorched.

There was joy throughout the school next day because the building was safe, and Billy Wakenshaw was acclaimed a hero.

One cannot help comparing this loyalty to a decrepit old building with the arson perpetuated frequently nowadays by pupils themselves, causing thousands of pounds worth of damage to their fine new fully-equipped schools.

23.

Once a pantomime was over the Drama Club members were eager to undertake the next one.

After the final performance of 'The Lost Totem', I left the stage clutching the lovely bouquet with which I had just been presented, feeling a great sense of release, looking forward to a rest and a little quiet routine. Then a small coyote touched my sleeve and asked, 'What is the next pantomime going to be, Miss?'

I said, 'I don't know. At the moment we'll just remember the last one and have a rest.'

But my imagination had been jerked into action as usual, and soon a little notebook was being filled with characters, scraps of dialogue, dance diagrams, song suggestions, plot-outlines in a confusion intelligible only to myself, and by the following September, 'Semina and the Dragon' was written and ready for auditions. These completed, the selected principals copied their parts in long-hand from the three typewritten scripts we possessed. Mr Bennington needed one for the lighting cues, Miss Hargreaves one for the music. Mr Crozier one for the scenery and as assistant-producer. I retained the original handwritten manuscript, which I allowed no-one to borrow.

During the autumn term there were routine rehearsals, building-up scene, sound and movement, but I had other preoccupations. Mr Soulsby had to re-enter hospital only a few days after our return from the summer vacation. He came back to school on October 14th, but was absent again from November 9th until December 15th when he struggled back because he hated to miss the end-of-term festivities, especially the Carol Service. His doctor was urging him to consider retirement.

Nevertheless, he was back at the helm after Christmas and, except for occasional days, continued until the second week in April, so in March he was at 'Semina and the Dragon' each evening, standing as usual in the foyer to

131

welcome past scholars and parents and to bid them good-night as they left. When they praised the performance he glowed with pride.

Knowing we had the facilities of Newlands School available, a more ambitious background was possible. By building up rostra and making full use of the lighting, we created a 'half-world' on a rugged mountain-top, inhabited by Dreams, Envies, Skeletons, a Dream-man, a Dragon and a little girl, Semina.

Semina and the Dragon are doomed to live there because she has always been selfish and he has always been afraid. They can only redeem themselves by overcoming their weaknesses.

Two gangsters arrive at the mountain top with sacks of stolen explosives. They have been instructed to wait there until their leader, Gaff, comes to pick up them and their booty. Unwittingly, they hide the explosives in the Dragon's tunnel. When the Dragon, accompanied by Semina, appears, they too retreat, in fear, into the tunnel.

News of the theft appears in the local press: grown-ups are concerned about the potential danger; the children would like the reward offered.

The Dream-man wishes to help Semina and the Dragon, so on Midsummer Eve, accompanied by the Dreams in their diaphanous draperies, he comes to the sleeping village children, among whom one boy Larry, who lives with his widowed mother and sister Lisette, is blind. Each child receives a dream which will urge him or her to the mountain top.

Next morning, pretending that Larry is King Arthur and the rest his knights and ladies, they set out for the summit. Larry cannot climb quickly because he has to feel his way and Lisette stays with him. The others decide to leave a paper trail for Lisette to follow. Short of material, they pick up the gangster's torn instructions, piece them together and read that the thieves have to signal their position with fire and smoke when the helicopter appears.

Realising the significance, they aim to capture the three gangsters and gain the reward so they climb quickly and reach the top despite sporadic attacks by Envies and Skeletons. They learn from Semina where the thieves and explosives are. They tell the Dragon to guard the tunnel while they go to signal Gaff to his doom. Semina, acting unselfishly for the first time, stays with the Dragon because he is so afraid, and when Larry and Lisette arrive she gives them a message from the others. Lisette goes to join them leaving Larry with Semina and the Dragon which has fallen asleep. The thieves peer out, grab Larry and Semina, put them in beside the explosives to use as hostages, and try to dodge past the sleeping Dragon. He is awakened by Semina's cries and her plight rouses his anger and courage. He breathes smoke and fire for the first time as he drives them back into the tunnel. Semina emerges but the Dragon's breath has ignited an explosive. Semina goes in to try to save Larry, there is a tremendous bang as they stagger out and fall flat.

Gaff is captured, Larry's sight restored by the shock and the reward gained by the children. Semina and the Dragon have redeemed themselves, she by unselfishness, he by courage. All ends in general rejoicing.

The Dragon costume was designed by Mr Crozier and constructed by the Needlework Club. It was green and scaly, and had a big paper-maché head with torch-bulb eyes and big nostrils. It was ingeniously constructed so that when the climax arrived the Dragon was able to switch on the red bulbs of his torch eyes and emit 'smoke' from his nostrils.

The fiery Dragon, and the explosive bang in the eerie half-light of the half world were most effective and duly applauded. The scenic effect throughout was quite striking.

I was to write one more pantomime script, but 'Semina and the Dragon' has always remained my own favourite. It has a beauty and mysticism which appeal to me, although its popularity lay in its scenic effects, dramatic climax, and the antics of the Knights and the Dragon.

A newspaper cutting recalls that 'the children delighted the audience with their assured acting.'

24.

During the summer term, Mr Soulsby decided he must retire at the end of the year and, in due course, submitted his resignation, then began to pester me to apply for the Headship. I knew I had no chance of success, as Deputy Heads were ineligible to become Head of their own school. He was sure there had been exceptions to this rule; he presented me with an unrequested and impossibly good testimonial and seemed to think it would be disloyal of me not to 'have a go'. Members of Staff individually urged me to send in an application, so eventually I wrote for the necessary form. The reply from the Education Office informed me briefly what I already knew – I was not eligible to apply.

Nevertheless I deeply appreciated the loyalty and esteem shown by my colleagues.

The pupils were unanimously sorry that 'the Gaffer', as he was affectionately known, was to leave and they began practical plans to express their esteem.

All too soon the last afternoon arrived. Press cuttings show a rather wistful Head receiving his parting gifts; a chiming clock presented by the Head Girl, Mavis Watson, on behalf of all the pupils, and a standard lamp with a carved plinth made by boys in the Woodwork Room.

Extract from newspaper

> ''The corridors of New Delaval Secondary Modern School echoed last week to three lusty cheers for the retiring Headmaster, Mr Sydney Soulsby, known affectionately by Staff and Scholars as ''the Gaffer.''

Later, there were private gifts as he bade the Staff farewell. His final entry in the Log Book, dated 21st December, 1956, reads:-

"Today ends my Headship of this School. I have spent some happy times here and am very grateful to Staff and Scholars for all their help.

I wish the new Headmaster, the Staff and Scholars "all the best" for 1957 and all the years ahead. May God guide this school family to a richer and fuller life.

And now to pastures new.

Sydney Soulsby."

It was the end of an era.

Nevertheless, Mr Soulsby's interest in the well-being of Delaval School never dimmed. He welcomed visits from teachers and pupils, appeared when he was able at school functions and never lost enthusiasm for life.

There was an improvement in his health after a time and for a few years he served as a councillor.

Even after a stroke which left him incapacitated and, later, blind, he remained cheerful and hopeful, always faithful to his school motto, 'Never Despair'.

The last time I saw him was in early Spring, 1981. My husband had returned home after a major operation. Mr Soulsby had asked his brother-in-law to bring him to see us, and he was led into our home tottering and blind, but carrying an armful of daffodils for me. Soon he was detailing his plans for the future: my husband was to select and classify some colour slides for him, he would supply the data, and I should write the book: a personal local history.

He died the following December, aged eighty-nine.

25.

The new Headmaster, Mr Gerald Kelly, had been a captain in the Army and after the war was in charge of the education of British children whose fathers were serving with the Army in Solingen, Western Germany.

On his return to Britain he joined the teaching staff at Newlands School. He became a member of the town council and, later, a magistrate.

He was a man of smart appearance with a military bearing, a short moustache, rather cold grey eyes and always well-dressed.

The school both gained and lost by his appointment: perhaps the balance struck was about right. We had been insular; he broadened our horizons and soon foreign holidays became a feature of school life. Journeys were made to Switzerland, France, Belgium and Germany. 'Twinning' with a school in Solingen began, so there was inter-pupil correspondence and exchange visits, with home-hospitality for visiting pupils and Staff in both countries. Foreign languages became part of the curriculum, French because it became a compulsory 'pilot-scheme' in Northumbrian schools, German because of its usefulness. It was taught by Mr Kelly himself to all classes; he spoke German fluently.

The scene became more formal, organization more obvious. There were official Staff meetings with an agenda; memoranda were circulated and duly signed. I became an intermediary between Staff and Headmaster. There was something of a military precision which made the 'family' feel of the school more difficult to sustain.

School uniform was introduced and failure to wear it publicly frowned upon. The majority conformed and soon navy blazers, grey skirts, white blouses, boys' grey trousers predominated, but there were always some rebels. All had always proudly worn school and House badges, the new ties proved popular, and girls enjoyed wearing gingham frocks in House colours during summer-time. they made these themselves in the Needlework Room. They were modern, individual in style, and well-cut.

But independence of character, amounting sometimes to stubbornness was a trait of the locality. Clothes of their own choice had often been so similar they looked uniform; blue jeans and donkey jackets a 'norm' for boys, but they disliked being told what they must wear. Over the years this occasioned some amusing incidents. One occurred not long before I retired. A petition reached Mr Kelly which he handed to me to deal with. It was headed, 'WE WANT TO WEAR TROUSERS'.

Then the signatures began. After it had been signed by twelve girls, a boy had got hold of it and the rest of the document was signed by boys!

I assembled the girls and explained that a demand would get them nowhere. I suggested that if one or two senior girls had approached Mr Kelly politely and explained why they would like trousers to be an alternative part of school uniform they might have had more success. 'By the way, why do you want to wear them in school?' I asked.

'To keep us warm. We freeze in school,' someone replied.

'Isn't that strange?' I said, 'A little while ago when some of you were wearing extremely short mini-skirts you told me it was because you were too hot in longer ones.'

Next morning when I arrived at school there seemed to be a buzz of excitement around the girls' cloakroom and it was matched by some indignation in the staffroom. A senior girl had arrived at school in a ruby-red, ankle-length velvet frock. What was I going to do about it?

'Nothing,' I replied, 'and I should like you to do the same. Ignore her appearance completely.'

Mr Kelly was attending Court that morning in his magisterial capacity so he knew nothing of the matter.

During the course of the morning the girls eyed me expectantly; the one in the red dress seemed to be just in front of me, or passing me on the stairs, whenever classes moved around. I ignored her completely until lunch-time when I saw her lingering on the landing. She began a slow descent as I ascended the stairs and we met in the middle. In fact, she nearly bumped into me. I smiled and said, 'What a pretty frock! Is the wedding this afternoon?'

She was in school uniform when the afternoon session began and we never saw the red dress again.

Mr Kelly had, perhaps of necessity, as great a prejudice in favour of school uniform. He treated petty theft with a milder rebuke than that accorded sartorial digression.

There was one troublesome boy who was against work himself and eager to disturb those who were industrious. With any weak teacher he was a pest. But his day of reckoning with Mr Kelly did not come until the morning he arrived at school wearing a crimson 'teddy-boy' suit. The Headmaster 'saw red' literally and metaphorically.

26.

A few events stand out from 1957, Mr Kelly's first year at Delaval.

In March, for the first time, the school acquired a secretary, Mrs Armstrong being appointed to come on two half-days each week; and on June 3rd we were allocated a typewriter! (Also new furniture for one classroom.)

The girls' netball team took part in the County Rally at Seaton Burn in April and reached third place in the table of results.

In June, the school won the Blyth Schools Sports Shield for Boys, although there were only seventy-six boys on the roll.

The traditional school trip, funded by pantomime profits, and now named the Annual Educational Excursion, went to Bowes Museum and Raby Castle in July.

The first official Parents' Evening took place in September and the production of the last pantomime I was to write, 'Triste de Mer', in November.

That year I relinquished, without regret, Physical Education classes and was installed as Religious Education teacher to the whole school. This was on the recommendation of the chief HMI when he visited the school in May. At the same time he suggested I might like to attend a national seven-day Religious Education Course to be held at Durham University in July.

I don't think I learned a great deal about teaching Religious Education, as the subject is officially known, but I recall the course with pleasure as a period of physical relaxation and mental stimulation.

Old Testament study was confined mostly to the book of Nehemiah, which seemed of limited use to a Secondary Modern teacher, but the lecturer, one of the Cathedral clergy, had a rich sonorous voice which brought out the full beauty of Biblical language. I should like to have heard him reading the Song of Songs, eg

"Rise up, my love, my fair one, and come away,
For lo, the winter is past, the rain is over and gone.
The flowers appear on the earth,
The time of the singing of birds is come,
And the voice of the turtle is heard in our land.''

or Ecclesiastes, eg 'To every thing there is a season...' etc., or some of the psalms.

New Testament study was rather eclectic; discussions aimed at separating fact from myth, an iconoclastic procedure which some members of the course seemed to find disturbing. But we did attend a synagogue service on the Saturday morning with an opportunity to ask the Rabbi questions afterwards. This occasion and the ensuing explanation of Jewish rites, customs and symbolism proved most useful afterwards.

There was an excursion to Housesteads where we walked along the Roman Wall and talked, discussing the influence of Roman supremacy on the spread of Christianity, enjoying the expansive view to north and south, and imagining how it must have felt to be a Roman soldier stationed there, especially in winter.

There were two free afternoons, which another member of the course invited me to spend with her exploring the countryside. She was a small demure-looking person, but her appearance was deceptive. She was a college Vice-Principal and daughter of a Congregational minister. She had a strong personality, a trenchant wit, and drove her small car extremely fast. She admitted that colleagues nicknamed her Jehu.

Her sense of direction was little better than mine which is infinitesimal. Once when she lost the way, I suggested stopping to ask someone for directions, but she said, 'I always find it quicker just to keep on driving until I find out where I am.' Consequently, we glimpsed the rural beauty of Durham at speed and, on my part, with some trepidation.

The evening meals were leisurely and good, followed by informal talks and interesting conversation.

There was some doctrinal prejudice. One of the Cathedral clergy, an old white-haired man with rosy cheeks and kind, wise eyes, suggested that everyone should participate in one Communion Service on the Sunday morning, but another Church of England ecclesiastic objected, so the sheep were separated from the goats for a brief period, the unconfirmed celebrating the sacraments at the nearest non-conformist chapel.

I returned to school after my week's absence physically and mentally rested, and was welcomed as though I had been away a long time.

There had been a bus strike during my sabbatical week. Staff living at a distance had arrived late; children who normally travelled by bus had, perforce, walked.

On the Friday, a teacher engaged in a 'Topical Talk' lesson with a junior class had asked, 'What happening this week has affected the daily-life of all of us?'

One child replied, 'Mrs Wrigley hasn't been to school all week.'

It was nice to have been away, but delightful to have been missed.

I spent a considerable amount of time thinking and assessing needs and circumstances before completing a Religious Education syllabus.

Most pupils had filled in imaginary forms as English exercises and had gathered facts in order to compile statistics in Mathematics lessons, so my questionnaire was accepted as normal and completed by all. From the results I found out which place of worship, if any, each one attended; how often; the last occasion; and when, if ever, apart from school assembly, they prayed. I also asked each one to write from memory the Lord's Prayer.

Some attended church or chapel regularly, going to Sunday School or morning service, rather more celebrated Christmas and Easter in a place of worship. The rest had been only to weddings and baptisms; a few had never been since their own baptism.

Not many prayed apart from school assembly although some admitted praying when afraid or when they wanted something badly.

The Lord's Prayer, in some instances, was astoundingly inaccurate, reminding me of a small boy I know of who returned from Sunday school one December morning and said they had sung the Cowboy Carol. This turned out to be 'Thus spake the Sheriff and forthwith...'

Faith is a stupendous thing and often elusive. Belief cannot be forced: reading a Bible can be a boring exercise for an adolescent; Bible stories no more than myths to their emerging cynicism. I always feel rather sorry for Shylock (*Merchant of Venice*) who in order to save his life and retain half his worldly goods must 'presently become a Christian'. What pathos there is in his 'I pray thee, give me leave to go from hence; I am not well. Send the deed after me and I will sign it.'

If Religious Education is to have any significance it must provide facts, evidence, stimuli to provoke thought and emotion from which faith may grow. A groundwork may be given, a pattern of prayer instilled, but for adolescents, as for the majority of people after the innocence of childhood is past, belief is personal, precious, and, for some, intermittent.

'I believe, help thou my unbelief.'

I found that young people could sometimes get a conception of faith by reading the 'Piper at the Gates of Dawn' chapter from 'Wind in the Willows' alongside Biblical extracts.

> "Lest the awe should dwell
> And turn your frolic to fret,
> You shall look on my power
> at the helping hour.
> But then you shall forget........forget."

To try to teach Religion is a great responsibility; to attempt it needs the full strength of a personal faith in a pure and non-denominational form; an ecumenical approach.

I decided the first essential was a concept of prayer as a line of communication with the Omnipotent (not a phrase I'd use with youngsters): prayer as a positive feeling of thanks for all good relationships and all the good things of life; prayer for directional guidance and moral strength, but never for selfish ends; prayer for the happiness and well-being of other people.

When we took the BBC Friday morning Service for Schools, everyone learned the Prayer for the Week from the BBC prayer card. The back section of RE notebooks was used for transcribing these prayers and for personal prayers. At the end of RE lessons we often said together, 'Please God, help me to forget my own wants and remember the needs of others.'

Secondly, to study the life of Jesus, his death and resurrection and his influence thenceforward relating it as far as possible to our own daily life. Thus Christmas was the celebration of Christ's birthday, gifts we received, his birthday gifts, parties his parties.

Between Christmas and Easter we read about Jesus' life as a Jewish boy maintaining Jewish tradition and customs as demonstrated in Old Testament history eg going up to Jerusalem for the Passover and Pentecost. The cross the girls cut on hot-cross-buns they made in Domestic Science lessons for Good Friday was a symbol of the crucifixion of Christ, who was sharing the form of capital punishment to which criminals of his day were doomed. The eggs that each family hardboiled, dyed and decorated to 'jarp', 'bool', and eventually eat on Easter Sunday, known locally as 'paste' eggs, were really Paschal eggs, signifying birth and new life, thence Christ living again.

144

At Whitsuntide, they imagined the Jews converging *en masse* to Jerusalem with their Pentecostal harvest offerings and hearing the news of the coming of the Holy Spirit from the excited disciples.

Thereafter, we dealt with the missionary work of the disciples: the life of Peter; the journeys of Paul; difficulties of transport and communication, hundreds of miles walked, letters carried by travellers to their destination; the satisfaction disciples gained from their commitment despite hardship and frustration; the selflessness and endurance of Christian pioneers.

There were lessons on miracles and parables. Pupils were encouraged to write modern parables based on their own everyday life as Christ's were based on his life and environment.

One year, in the parish magazine of St Bede's Church, Newsham, a prize was offered for a modern parable. A number of pupils submitted entries and one girl won the prize, which was presented by a Franciscan monk from Alnmouth at a school morning assembly. I'm afraid most of the children were so intrigued by his bare feet and brown habit that they didn't really listen to his wise and simple talk.

The Vicar sent me a note of thanks for the entries submitted by the school and a book about the parables which he thought I might like to borrow. It was written in very erudite English with copious quotations in Latin and Greek. There is something dismaying about clergymen who do not seem to understand the simple spiritual needs of ordinary human beings.

Two examples immediately come to mind

I was at Conway one Whitsuntide when all the children from a local camp for schools were taken to Morning Service at Conway Church. The captive congregation numbered several hundred and the whole of a lengthy abstruse sermon was devoted to deciding whether the Holy Spirit should be called 'He' or 'It'.

The other occasion was nearer home. The local Vicar asked if a manger could be constructed in the Woodwork Room to erect outside the church as background for an Advent Nativity Scene. My husband deliberately chose for the task a group of boys he thought might benefit from the experience. The finished manger, rough-hewn, sturdily-constructed, looked authentic and had entailed real endeavour. He 'phoned the Vicar and asked when it would be convenient to bring the manger and erect it; an appointment was duly made.

The boys carried the manger to the church and my husband went to the Vicarage, expecting the vicar to come out and encourage the boys with his appreciation. Instead, he was given a message that the Vicar was busy but would they just get on with the job. The boys completed the work and came away obviously disappointed by their reception. Thus an evangelical opportunity was missed, indicating a lack of human perception.

Old Testament lessons outlined the growth of the Jewish nation from the time of Abraham; prophetic vision; tribal offering and spontaneous awareness of God; the institution of rules and laws so that each must consider the welfare of the many; personalities of outstanding influence; selected psalms, proverbs and other Biblical poems.

Spontaneous drama, especially if a whole year group is involved, is useful in Religious Education, provided the free acting is unobtrusively directed and controlled; eg a tribe, wandering in the desert, camp for the night. The men put up the goatskin tents, the women fetch water in goatskin bags, children help to round-up, feed and water the animals. Suitable animals are selected for slaughter for the evening meal, one being burnt as an offering to God. As the smoke rises and disperses in the desert air, they feel their offering, their sharing of food, reaching God, all-pervading in space.

I remember one little blonde boy who insisted on being the sacrificial lamb.

There was a memorable Pentecostal rendering by a young year group developing over several lessons. It gradually and spontaneously grew to a lively, involved occasion, additional props arriving fortuitously. There were gipsy-type salespeople, wayward animals, flaunting rich, pious poor, baskets of fruit and vegetables, but always the culmination of offering and spiritual joy at eventide in Jerusalem.

Prayers and selective Bible study might suffice to meet the needs of some pupils, but extra material was needed to reach adolescents, especially those with little or no home background of religion. With such seniors I concentrated on readings about people whose faith had brought them personal happiness and helped them to endure adversity: enabled them to work selflessly for the well-being of others: eg Dr Albert Schweitzer; Father Damian; Mother Theresa; Toyohika Kagara of Japan; Gladys Aylward, 'The Small Woman'. The morning after the latter was the subject of an Eamonn Andrews' 'This is your Life' programme, there were pupils meeting me at the gate to ask if I had seen it.

The morning after her death was announced, they waited quite sadly to tell me, though, as one fifteen-year-old lad remarked, 'But she was sixty-one years old, miss, so she'd had a good innings.' As I was sixty myself by then I could not fully appreciate his philosophy.

With the senior classes I also read extracts from books such as Arthur Grimble's *Pattern of Islands* where the natives instinctively and fervently pray for blessings and peace for loved ones at time of crisis, and where the RC missionary risked his life and his chance of the last sacraments to take them to a dying man on another island.

Hilary's *The Last Enemy* which is death, and his vision in hospital of a dying friend. The Story of Janis Babson – the Canadian child who faced leukaemia with great courage, had a vision of life beyond death, and insisted that her eyes should be donated to an eye bank. As a result many Canadians made the same kind of bequest, including a contingent of the Canadian Mounties. Moreover, because of her life-story, a centre for research into leukaemia was established in Palestine.

In addition to this normal Religious Education syllabus Mr Kelly encouraged greater involvement of Staff and pupils in the morning service, each House being made responsible in turn for one week's programme. A teacher compiled the material, rehearsed the Bible-reading and a suitable secular reading with two pupils, selected the hymns, spoke the linking sentences, and said the closing prayer.

I hope our united endeavours, however inadequate, had some influence for good and happiness in the adult lives of those we taught.

27.

Although compiling the Religious Education syllabus, and preparing myself to teach it, preoccupied me during 1957, rehearsals went ahead as usual during Drama Club sessions, during lunch breaks and after school for 'Triste de Mer, the Mermaid Without a Tail'. The staging of this pantomime tested the ingenuity and resourcefulness of Mr Crozier, the Woodworkers and the Needlework Club to the full.

It was the story of a human child living with sea creatures in the depth of the ocean.

The Neptune twins, Ebb and Flow, had each been given a seahorse as a seventh birthday present. They were riding up and down on them in the ocean when they saw an earth-child tumbling in from the light. She had no fins, no tail and she felt warm. Neither of them had touched an earth-being before. They swam home with the frightened little girl, and their parents, Queen Peril and King Sargasso, decided to keep her as a pet, a mermaid without a tail, although they hoped one would grow. They named her Triste de Mer.

She is cherished by the mermaids and desired by the Octopuses who want to squeeze her in their tentacles and eat her. The sea-scene is also inhabited by the Oogles

> ''... the joy of the sea,
> The shimmer and glint on the top of the water,
> The murmur and movement of smooth summer
> light;
> They dart and they dance to the top of the water.''

They represent the constant movement of the sea and are alert to all happenings.

SMILER REMEMBERS

The village children dive into the sea one day wearing snorkels and flippers. The Oogles report seeing them; the mermaids with Ebb and Flow swim to investigate and, after a struggle, capture eight children and take them to the Neptunes. Ebb and Flow promise to feed and scrub them every day if allowed to keep them as pets. King Sargasso decides to put them in a humanarium and charge a brass button a visit and a seed pearl extra to see the Mermaid without a Tail.

Seastar, the most beautiful mermaid, is sorry for Triste de Mer, who always looks sad. She risks swimming to land as the moon rises. There she sees the young fisherman, Tim, who agrees to dive down for Triste de Mer.

Meanwhile, Ebb and Flow have tired of looking after the humans and agree to free them when the children promise to give them buttons of pearl, glass, brass and bone from clothing they have at home in exchange for their freedom. The twins swim to land with their captives to fetch the buttons, the children having promised to throw water on them to keep them wet.

Eventually, a friendship is established between humans and sea-creatures. The pantomime ends with a procession of sea-creatures, led by King and Queen Neptune, coming to take part in the festivities at the Fishermen's Gala.

All goes well until a maroon is fired to announce the beginning of the firework display. The sea-creatures singing, in canon, 'Land is burning' (to the tune of 'London's burning') retreat swiftly to the ocean depths, leaving the humans wondering if what they had experienced is real, or only a dream.

The harbour scene was easily adapted from props already to hand, but the sea-scene was another matter which was eventually simply and adequately solved. We made a draw-curtain big enough to cover the whole front of Newlands stage, in fine nylon net. When spotlights probed it, the background, (Neptune's palatial cavern hung with seaweeds, decorated with shells and furnished with pieces of wreck) was clearly visible, and sound was not impeded by it. To it Mr Crozier fastened in haphazard fashion, cut-outs of marine artefacts. Suitable changing colour was provided by the lighting.

The old well-worn cat-suits came out again for the octopuses with extra stiffened feelers and tentacles attached.

The mermaids looked attractive in pale blue and green bodice-tops trimmed with 'seaweed' and trousers tapering to the ankle where long pointed ends gave the impression of a tail. The material was dappled with silver paint and stitching to simulate scales.

The Oogles, the smallest girls in the school, wore pastel-coloured costumes designed like a one-piece bathing suit but with a roundness of appearance, the aim being to make them look like bubbles of light.

The Woodworkers provided Neptune (Brett Smith) with a huge trident which he used very effectively. He and his wife contributed much to the humour of the play. He was a lean slenderly-built lad with pointed features and ginger hair. Queen Peril, tall and well-built, overwhelmed him. Though furtively sarcastic about her, he cringed from her verbal and physical onslaught. A press photograph shows him peering impishly over his trident.

A few years ago Brett called to see us, looking smart and alert in RAF uniform, the red hair and pointed features unmistakeable. His casting as King Neptune had fortuitously been apt; he gained his County Colours (Northumberland) rowing for the RAF in 1975 and was in the national RAF crew at Henley in 1975 and 1976. He also swam for the RAF.

Pantomime rehearsal-week had for the Staff a different atmosphere from earlier occasions, although among the pupils there was the usual excitement and joie de vivre.

I asked Mr Kelly for permission to depart from the timetable in order to devote the five afternoons, which included two rehearsals at Newlands, to the pantomime. He agreed, a little reluctantly, requesting me to make a temporary timetable ensuring that those not involved were being suitably taught. I could not adequately explain that, in spirit, everyone was involved, like a family preparing for Christmas. To anyone with a keen sense of order and precision, our diverse and simultaneous pursuits must have seemed chaotic – little groups of players in corners rehearsing dialogue; dancers going through routines in the corridors; choruses practising around the piano; entrances, exits and groupings being directed; individuals going to try-on costumes; scenery being humped around, knocked together and painted in any available space. The tension of knowing the first performance was so near made everyone more talkative.

There is something about the hub-bub if you are part of it; a oneness of purpose at the heart of the apparent chaos, but, seen and heard objectively, it must have been irritating to a military man.

Nevertheless, coherence was reached by the end of the week and the final rehearsal. Scenery and props were in place or in readiness at Newlands, the costumes pressed and hung or packed, make-up trays in order and tickets sold.

There were capacity audiences and complimentary press notices, one mentioning

'this old colliery village school, with no assembly hall or stage, but their

Drama Club produces some of the most exciting school pantomimes in the area.

This year's 'Triste de Mer', with a cast of sixty-five, had its première at Newlands, a neighbouring modern school with its own theatre.'

It concluded as follows

'When the pantomime's run is over, Mrs Wrigley will start writing again for next year.'

But she didn't. Instead, we decided to go back to the beginning of the cycle and do previous productions again, merely bringing topical allusions up to date. After all each had only had public showing for one week at most.

Over the ensuing years this proved a popular move, and, eventually, some mothers and fathers who had been participants in earlier years were coming backstage at the end of the show with their offspring. We even had a few second generation performers by 1970.

Mr Kelly came to one performance of 'Triste de Mer', complimented pupils and Staff in assembly on the success of their endeavour, and was gratified by the profits, but we couldn't help missing the enthusiastic participation of 'the Gaffer'.

28.

I believe the spirit of a school matters more than its architecture or appurtenances. If a feeling of corporate oneness can be achieved; if pupils and Staff relate sympathetically; if the school is not regarded as an establishment doling out compulsory instruction, but, rather an entity encouraging loyalty, unity of purpose, and endeavour, then the educational process may be said to have begun. Delaval School was fortunate in the number of its teachers dedicated to this end.

Despite its dilapidation and inconveniences, it maintained a steadfast Staff over a period of years, until a series of changes began in 1958 and Domestic Science suffered first.

Mrs Gillespie, who had been teaching Domestic Science and Needlework, resigned. Mrs Pearson, a part-time teacher, undertook the Needlework classes and, in due course, was employed full-time. She stayed until 1967 and her efficiency as a teacher and her own good dress-sense were reflected throughout that time in the garments and accessories which the girls made. Every girl in the school could use a sewing-machine with ease and accuracy; not one failed to produce satisfactorily completed pieces of work – unlike me in my early schooldays.

The mannequin parades she staged were appreciated by parents and friends. The most ambitious was in 1963, Education Year, as part of a special Open Day, organised by Mr Kelly, when the school was open for any member of the public to walk in, look around, and see the pupils at work. Numerous visitors took advantage of the opportunity.

As well as the mannequin parade there were displays of country-dancing and fencing, an exhibition of completed articles in the Woodwork Room, and boys working on their garden plots or in the greenhouse stocked with tomatoes, pot plants and seedlings. Classes giving their competitive 'talks' had much

153

larger audiences than usual, and experiments in progress in the Science Room drew interested spectators.

The *Blyth News* gave a full account of the afternoon and included a picture of five of the mannequins. They modelled dresses, blouses and skirts, trouser-suits and one fully-lined winter coat. Mrs Pearson is quoted as saying, 'The object is to demonstrate how cheaply modern garments can be made, and also how fashionable school-clothing can be.'

For three months there was no Domestic Science teacher at all. Then came a succession of short-stay teachers, stability only being restored four years later when Miss Grace Connacher came. She was still participating fully in the life of the school, when I retired.

The most memorable Staff change of 1958, however, was the retirement, in July, of Mr Robinson, after forty-five years as a teacher, thirty of them spent at New Delaval. He had taught Geography and Mathematics to successive generations, so past pupils occasionally made up a complete family, mother, father and children. His departure was especially regretted by the girls: it was akin to losing a favourite uncle.

A press photograph reveals some of them weeping as they watch his retirement presentation from the front rows of seats in the New Delaval Miners' Welfare Hall.

His official gift from Staff and scholars, past and present, was a leather wallet containing a cheque, but the items he especially treasured were handmade. Senior boys had made a set of turned oak egg cups on an oak platter, and the girls a linen tablecloth on which each had embroidered her own name as part of the design.

His post was not filled until October when Mr Sam Haley came, giving renewed strength to the establishment and helping to foster the 'family' spirit. He is a man with a deep respect for learning and hates to see educational opportunities wasted; he is also truly human with a volatile temper. He gives enthusiasm and complete involvement to whatever he attempts, whether it be teaching Geography and Literature or home-brewing and playing billiards. Interest in the two latter pursuits he shared with my husband. He became friend as well as colleague to both of us, along with his wife Margaret, and later, their daughter and son; a friendship still firm more than twenty years on.

Mrs Rockcliffe became part of the permanent staff in 1958 too and stayed for about four years. Pupils will remember her for visits to London which she organised, especially one in June 1960, when she and Mr Bennington took thirty-six children by private coach to spend a week there. With their own bus to transport them daily, they were able to complete a packed itinerary – St. Paul's; Westminster Abbey; Tower of London; Kew Gardens; Science Museum; Natural History Museum; Regent's Park; Madame Tussaud's; Horse Guards' Parade; shopping in Kensington High Street. But the highlights were being members of the audience at a BBC broadcast, and being conducted round the Houses of Parliament by Mr N Dodds, MP, this visit having been arranged for them by Mr Robens, then Chairman of the National Coal Board but formerly Member of Parliament for Blyth.

Mr Kelly organised and led the foreign tours himself. A good percentage of pupils took advantage of them and benefited from them, and sufficient teachers were always available to help. My husband and I went once, the year of the World Fair in Brussels, when the ultimate destination was Davos, in Switzerland.

We crossed by boat to Ostend and spent two nights in the Youth Hostel there, so that a visit could be made to the Brussels Exhibition – my first experience of Youth-Hostelling. The sleeping accommodation was stark, Mrs Kelly and myself with fourteen girls locked in a relatively small room with tiered bunk beds. The washing-facilities were even more bleak – rows of sinks in the basement, each with a cold water tap and no privacy.

Most of the party went to Brussels, but I stayed behind with four girls who did not wish to go.

After a meagre breakfast of dark bread with cheese or jam, the bus party departed. Then I was told that no one was allowed in the hostel during the day, but an exception had been made so that the five of us could go in for lunch between twelve and one o'clock. Then we were locked out. (During the night we had been locked in!)

However, it was a beautiful sunny morning and the girls were content to bathe, play on the beach and watch the shrimp-gatherers.

By mid-day the sky was overcast, and by the time we had eaten our unappetising lunch of dry dark bread and cheese, and were again locked out, rain was falling relentlessly.

I was wondering where we could find shelter until the doors were re-opened at five o'clock when I noted an aeroplane hovering preparatory to landing. The airport! That would do. We soon caught a bus which took us there and we spent a relatively pleasant afternoon on the covered terrace eating ice cream and watching arrivals and departures.

The evening meal was a repetition of the lunch menu, plus soup.

I was glad next morning to board a train to Basle. There the overnight accommodation and food were good and our stay too brief in such an interesting city.

The ensuing train journey to Davos took us through picturesque lake and mountain-scenery, and our hotel, near the little railway station of Davos Plats, was delightful, with gentle fir-clad slopes behind, a stream and steep Alpine slope patterned with flowers in front, and warm hospitality within. The chef pandered to the insular tastes of our youngsters, providing 'cheeps' as part of the generous evening meals. There was space for dancing and games.

The days were spent in excursions by rail to Klosters and St Moritz, walking, climbing, riding in cable cars and on chair-lifts – and shopping! Children are always inveterate shoppers. On any excursion, be it ten miles from home or a thousand, for an hour or for a fortnight, once free, they make for shops with ant-like concentration. At Davos, pocket-money was meted out in daily instalments; otherwise most would have been penniless after the second day.

The holiday was an enjoyable experience and such excursions enable teachers and pupils to enjoy a more relaxed relationship than is feasible in school. But my husband and I had always devoted quite a lot of leisure-time to school pursuits and we liked to keep the long summer vacation to ourselves, to relax, to follow pursuits and hobbies in a leisurely way, to visit friends, and to wander with our car, and sometimes a tent, in Britain or on the Continent, without a rigid timetable and with a flexible itinerary. Thereby, we could return to school each September relaxed mentally and recharged physically, able to face the year ahead with application and enthusiasm; so we did not join in any further foreign holidays.

Another retirement took place sadly in 1963 when Miss Hargreaves decided to accept an ill-health pension.

Throughout her teaching career she suffered from migraine, seldom a week passing without an attack incapacitating her for at least half a day. As the years passed, her absences due to this ailment became more frequent and of longer duration. We shared her classes among us and coped as best we could.

She was sturdily-built, had close-cropped hair, clear cut features and a beautiful natural complexion. She always wore tweed suits, shirt-blouses, and flat well-polished walking shoes. Her healthy and almost masculine appearance entirely belied her temperament as she was hypersensitive and artistic. She was punctilious about the smallest details and easily upset by minor incidents; her feelings could be hurt unwittingly by chance remarks.

Much of her life seemed lived in a state of tension, yet she played the piano beautifully: she interpreted Chopin especially with delicacy and feeling.

She was loyal and hardworking, and without her the pantomimes would not have been possible. There were anxious moments just before the actual performances, as sometimes she was not available for all the final rehearsals. On such occasions, we used a tape-recorder to rehearse dances and sang as best we could without accompaniment. But she was always there on the night.

Everyone was sorry that her career should end so early, but it was the only way in which her personal problem could be met. Her break with school-life was complete: there was no contact with pupils or Staff thereafter. Perhaps this was best for her, and there was no ill-will. Indeed we felt sad for her and wished her well.

There was no other member of Staff who could play the piano well and no specially-trained music teacher, yet our luck held out. There was never a year when we were unable to present a pantomime with a pianist in full musical control, assisted loyally, right to the end, by Ivan with his drums and Mr Taylor with his violin.

The first to take over was Mr Laurie Farrell; who came from industry into teaching, and stayed with us for three years. He could play several brass instruments as well as being an accomplished pianist. His father was conductor of Ashington Colliery Band. He joined me in running the Drama Club and I was able to leave the musical side entirely to him. He could extemporise and change keys to fit voices in a most useful way.

He moved on at a time when the Maths post became vacant. It was filled by Mr David Pope, a young teacher who related well to our youngsters. He had a modern outlook and played the guitar as well as the piano. He gave time, skill and enthusiasm unstintingly to the Drama Club: the success of Delaval's final pantomime owed much to him.

For some years, the Old Scholars' Association had been in abeyance, except for occasional social evenings, but had never been officially wound up. Then, at the beginning of the sixties, official youth clubs attached to schools came into being and youth leaders were appointed, usually from the Staff of the relevant school. Consequently, in May 1961, there was a meeting of New Delaval Secondary Modern School's Management Committee, attended by Miss V Tully, the County Youth Organiser, to set up a Youth Club for Fourth Year pupils and past-pupils. Mr Crozier was appointed leader and a committee elected comprising four school governors, two parents' representatives and three co-opted members. Mr Kelly became secretary and I was treasurer. It was at this juncture that we transferred the funds of the original club to the new one.

Miss Ann Martin had come to the school as a Physical Education teacher in 1960 and she became assistant leader.

There were forty-three members at the Club's first evening session on 15th June: it progressed successfully and maintained its strength.

Miss Martin stayed for six years, during which time the girls profited from having a properly trained PE teacher at last, one who combined teaching-craft with personal enthusiasm. She entered so much into the life of the school that even after she left she seemed a part of it, turning-up on all social and official occasions. She came to our retirement party and still calls to see me sometimes.

The next change came 1965–1966, when a new type of Youth Work and Adult Education was inaugurated. A Further Education and Youth Tutor was appointed to each senior school to run a Youth Centre and organize and supervise Adult Education classes. These tutors were accorded Deputy Head status, worked on a part-time basis in school during the day, especially as Careers Officers, and spent four evenings and some weekends doing Youth Work and running Adult Evening Classes. A wide variety of hobbies and leisure pursuits were made available, and training done for the Duke of Edinburgh Award Scheme.

Mr Crozier became the Tutor for Delaval School and Mr Bennington left to take up a similar post at Haydon Bridge. No one could have been more worthy of such promotion, but we were sad to say farewell. Mr Bennington had been a popular teacher for eighteen years and contributed much to the spirit of the school. He had gone straight from his own schooldays into the wartime Royal Navy. He suffered a bad spinal injury in action but, after a year in hospital, made a full and remarkable recovery, did a teacher-training course and came to his first post, New Delaval, in 1948.

He was succeeded by other friendly and efficient Maths teachers but no one could fully replace his contribution to the vitality of the school.

I cannot close this chapter without mention of two others, Mrs Helen Young and Mr Tony Gray.

Mrs Young first came as a supply teacher on one of the rare occasions when I was absent, ill with laryngitis, so I did not meet her. When I returned, my Form greeted me with pleasure. They were glad I was back! A new teacher had 'towered over them' and apparently spoken with some authority.

Soon afterwards Mrs Young became a part-time member of Staff. I found she was slim, smart and not many inches taller than I am and certainly shorter than some of her cowed critics. She took over PE when Miss Martin left, taught junior Maths, and entered fully into the varied aspects of school-life with the force of her personality.

School numbers increased as the school leaving-age was again raised and a Fifth Form established. My husband gave up teaching Woodwork to concentrate on Gardening and Biology and Mr Gray came as Woodwork teacher. He had a common-sense approach to his subject and was a friendly but firm disciplinarian. The boys continued to produce useful well-constructed articles and acquired an ability to make and mend which would serve them well in adult life. He coached football and gave spontaneous assistance to after-school projects. He was one of the 'family'.

29.

If this had been the story of a building, and not of a community, it would have ended with the events of 1965.

In this year the building of a new Blyth Grammar School at Bebside was completed and occupied. The Local Education Authority decided to close the little Infant School at New Delaval, move the children into our building after suitable alterations had been made, and transfer our pupils *en bloc* to the old Grammar School; the place where I had spent six years myself as a scholar.

The move was made with a minimum of disruption at the end of the year.

Mr Dagg, the LEA's Stores Officer came on 7th December and made arrangements for equipment and furniture to be moved on the ensuing 22nd and 23rd.

The place was a hive of activity for the final fortnight of term. All desks, cupboards and drawers had to be cleared, the accumulation of years to be disposed of, or stored for future use. Discarded old-fashioned text-books were perused with derisory scorn by young helpers, and odd copies taken home: some had names of forebears on the fly-leaf.

Exercise books were fastened in bundles; books in current use counted and put into packing cases; tools, writing implements and assorted equipment into other containers. Sorting the contents of my own cupboard was like dusting my bookshelves at home – more reading than dusting. I kept pausing to read specimens of pupils' work I had forgotten I had kept. Some I burnt, but a few I could not bear to part with.

Included in the activity of this period were two evenings devoted to the Junior and Senior Christmas parties, and, on 20th December, an afternoon Carol Service in St Bede's Church. The service was approved by the Vicar but devised and presented by the pupils themselves: traditional carols linked by

Bible readings and original poems. The Vicar said a prayer and pronounced the final benediction.

On 22nd December, books and equipment were moved, and on the following day, the last day of term, the furniture went. Soon the old building was empty of people and contents, but, for me full of memories, as I took a final walk around classrooms, the crossed corridors, venue of assemblies for twenty-one years, and the garden with its bare trees, lawns, empty vegetable plots and faded residue of autumn flowers. I knew it would always be for me a place of nostalgic recall.

The Grammar School, thenceforward to be officially known as Delaval School, had been vacant for a few months prior to our moving. It had been kept clean and ventilated but minor repairs were required. There were water leaks and bursts in the Annexe Gymnasium and the Woodwork and Technical Drawing rooms. Mr Kelly had a busy Christmas holiday ensuring that essential repairs were completed.

On 10th January, 1966, we assembled in our new school, Headmaster, 232 pupils, and ten full-time and one part-time teacher. We had a small hall, a gymnasium, Science, Woodwork, Domestic Science, Needlework, Art, Medical Inspection and Projection rooms, a fine Library and more classrooms than we could fill. There were separate playing-fields for boys and girls, tennis and netball courts, and a school-garden to which the greenhouse from the old school had been transferred. The rooms were light and spacious.

By the end of the first day, we had restored all paraphernalia to its appointed storage space and begun to stamp our separate personalities on our respective classrooms. I delighted in the bookcases with clear glass doors which stretched all along one wall of my room. I love books to be seen all the time. Soon boys came round with plants from the greenhouse to put on the wide window-sills. I put a vase of flowers on the low table of polished wood which replaced the high old fashioned teacher's desk of former years.

We were still Delaval, but in a fine new school.

The Library was outstanding. It had been built as a memorial to Miss Iris Murdoch, the good intellectual Scotswoman who was Headmistress when I was a pupil there: she had died of cancer in early middle-age. It was panelled in dark oak, had dark oak shelves, tables, chairs and steps, and tall windows overlooking the playing fields.

Over the years we had amassed a good collection of books; fiction; non-fiction; sets of encyclopedias, as there had always been a generous library allowance. We had always encouraged private reading but also tried to instill respect for books. They had been kept in good repair.

We now had a librarian worthy of the library. Mr Haley had been a librarian before entering the teaching profession and it became his special concern. Fiction was arranged alphabetically, according to author; non-fiction according to subject; encyclopedias and other reference books accorded their own easily-accessible space.

He catalogued all the books and put cards, with cross-references, into a filing cabinet. He taught senior pupils to use the system and act as librarians. He vigilantly maintained order and upkeep, and, as new books were added annually, a fine range was soon available to suit all tastes – and to provide material for research and information.

The pupils loved the playing fields and were quite new-fangled by the spaciousness of the school and its sophisticated facilities. Yet it took them sometime to get used to it, as indeed it did me. There was light and space, but a housing estate had grown around the school, and our gates opened on to a main road. Pupils had to remain within the grounds during recreational periods, whereas at Delaval 'up the Laverick' had been an unofficial extension of their otherwise impossibly small playing area. They had been able to hear the school bell from the pit ponds and the edge of the heaps. It was several weeks before they could be completely restrained from wandering out casually along the road.

When summer came, I took Literature classes to the end of one playing field where there were a few trees and we could lean against the wooden fence and read, but it didn't have the same sense of space and freedom. It enabled one to understand the discontent experienced by families moved from slum dwellings to modern housing estates. Actually, of course, like them, in all practical ways, we were much better off, but no one now brought a baby shrew for me to look at or took me over to the pond to see fledglings in a nest.

There was a new formality in school-life. Visitors called to see us, but they ceased to 'drop-in'. The old building had been a focal point in the neighbourhood for past pupils with time on their hands. They did not disturb lessons, they just sat-in: a pit boy on night-shift; an off-duty nurse; a shop-assistant on early-closing day; a shipyard apprentice on strike. Sometimes they requested work to do or books to read to aid them in preparation for an examination. One boy asked Mr Bennington for Mathematics questions, regretting he had not been more diligent at school. But our new premises were in a different locality and past pupils would have felt intruders had they called casually.

Those who did come were usually from a more distant past and working away from the area. They came specifically to renew acquaintance.

One such visit surprised a junior class engaged in an RE lesson. There was a knock at the door and a tall athletic, blazer-clad man entered, shook hands with me, said he was home for a few days and had called to see how I was. There was a nudging silence and a sense of keen awareness in the room. The man was Brian Williamson, recognised by the boys as a footballer with a First Division team.

30.

The five years leading up to 1970 saw an acceleration in the changing social attitudes which had been growing over the past decade. The change was not local, it was a national, in fact an international phenomena, a youth cult marked by obsessive materialism, antagonism to rules and authority, and aggressiveness.

I disagree with those who attribute it to poverty and bad housing-conditions. In earlier years, large Delaval families had been reared happily despite poor wages and no strike pay, in the long rows of colliery houses with no bathroom nor indoor lavatories. Baths were taken in galvanised tin baths in front of kitchen fires, the water heated in big pans or a boiler at one side of the fireplace. The used water had to be ladled into buckets and carried to outside sinks. I did this myself in my teens nightly. There was something very cosy about bathing in the firelight, even though the preparation and clearing away were tedious. I did not live in a house with a bathroom until I was thirty. I remember the replacement of earth closets by water closets, still in the backyard, as a luxurious innovation.

During lengthy miners' strikes the odour of baking herring characterised walks along the colliery rows, as these fish were very cheap. These and homemade soup, made from bones and homegrown vegetables, were staple foods in hard times. Bread was always home-baked. Children fetched flour and yeast from a grocer's and big earthenware crocks of dough were set to rise on the burnished steel fenders in front of small-coal fires. Crusty bread, spiced loaves, currant or caraway-seed teacakes, and girdle scones had a texture and flavour far superior to the fare displayed today in super-markets and extolled in TV advertisements, and they are still more satisfying and considerably cheaper. Moreover, there is a mental soothing in kneading dough and carrying out other processes of home-baking.

In the first quarter of the century children sometimes went barefoot of necessity. Now clothing allowances are discreetly available to the truly needy.

By 1950 many colliery houses had been replaced by modern semi-detached with all mod-cons, and living-conditions had been improved in most of the remaining old houses.

I do not fundamentally blame the young for their violence and aggression though I could never condone their behaviour. They had, and still have, insidious influences to cope with. Material possessions have become apparent signs of personal worth, the lack of them a measure of failure. To own cameras, record players, portable TV's, transistor radio sets, videos, matters more than using them. As miners' wages improved they were able to provide their offspring with such status symbols and usually did.

As more married women went out to work and men's wages increased, extra money altered the pattern of home-life. Men spent more of their leisure in working-men's clubs; their wives went to bingo. Their children, amply provided with pocket money, were left to their own devices more than ever before. The latch-key era had begun.

The common attitude to crime altered: to be found out mattered more than the theft itself. Honesty in words and dealing didn't seem as praiseworthy as clever evasions.

Puberty came earlier and with it the anxieties, urgencies and complexities of adolescence, all made more difficult by the enveloping commercialism and the mores of the new 'permissive' society. Children's fantasies grow from their environment; from what they see and hear. They experiment by imitating – smoking being one obvious example.

The TV screen became a reservoir of spurious simulation: sexual activities becoming increasingly explicit, plays making infidelity, abnormality and violence seem commonplace and therefore more easily acceptable. Clever criminal strategies and violence (often in the cause of justice) inspired admiration and imitation. Advertisements made happiness, glamour, beauty and virility seem easily available to those with enough money to buy the right commodities. Moreover, the TV screen has promoted in most of us a certain insensitivity. We feel concern and compassion as we watch bombing of cities, maiming of children, people and animals dying of hunger and thirst, but we go on eating our supper.

The general attitude to work altered, maybe because work became more impersonal and less self-satisfying. To win the pools and never work again became a weekly objective in many households. The same attitude had now to be striven against in school: many attended daily 'against work' on principle, without really knowing why, and it became increasingly difficult to arouse the interest which brings out the best in pupils. The permissive society had begun: the prostitution of the Absolutes; Beauty; Truth; Love; Freedom, was becoming confused with self-indulgence; Liberty with licentiousness.

These general trends debased relationships in schools too. Nevertheless, although the 'needling' of teachers became something of a creative art, there was only a small minority of trouble-raisers at Delaval, and these could be contained. Teaching, however, lost some of its joy, if none of its challenge.

The pervading influence of TV and radio gave added importance to the spoken word, so, in teaching, we tried to meet this trend.

By this time we had a small Fifth Year, all candidates for the newly-inaugurated CSE Examination and Oral English was an integral part of this, each candidate being required to converse for about ten minutes with an outside examiner who visited the school for this purpose.

In preparation for this, I used to have discussion periods when I would suggest an opening topic to set them going and then let the conversation open out, trying to ensure that everyone took part and that speech was grammatical and clearly-enunciated, but otherwise staying in the background. Their fluency improved and I think giving expression to their thoughts and emotions helped them too: it certainly gave me an inkling of the yearnings and perplexities of their generation. Few looked with hope or purpose to a distant future and they were bored with the monotony of the present. They tried to overcome hopelessness and an inexplicable inherent loneliness with group activity and a manipulated excitement: hence the gang-warfare; the aggression; the destruction and violence. These feelings are reflected in the sad monotony and strident clamour of their songs.

The Fifth Form enjoyed their discussion periods and, at times, feelings ran high; arguments developed and had to be contained. Just before the interviews for the 1970 Oral English Examination I briefed each examinee. To one lad, who when really worked up would ejaculate 'Why, man!' and also let slip the odd expletive, I said, 'Remember not to call her 'Man' and don't swear.'

He came out smiling, looked affectionately down at me, and said, 'I didn't call her 'Man' and I only said 'bloody' once.' I think there was more teasing than truth in this: anyway, he gained a First Class pass.

The school also participated in two television programmes.

As an English exercise, some pupils wrote to Alderman Gilbert Barker, Chairman of the Town Parks Committee, suggesting ways in which Blyth foreshore could be improved. As a result, two girls were interviewed in the *Look North* programme, and two girls and four boys invited to take part in the Tyne Tees topical programme, *Spotlight*.

Mr Les Barratt, the programme director came to school to select them and to brief them. Two were to prepare a geographical description of the lay-out of the town; two to prepare a report on the misuse of public amenities and two to explore prospects of Blyth as a holiday resort.

The rest of the year-group were invited to be members of the audience along with Mr Kelly, my husband and myself. It was a novel experience taking part in the preliminary 'run-up', seeing the cameras swinging and angling into action, appreciating the professionalism and exhibitionism. Afterwards refreshments were provided and a social half-hour ensued. I remember conversing with one ITV man and asking him why they broadcast so many poor 'westerns'. He replied, somewhat cynically, that it was to enable him to maintain his sons at public schools. His job depended on successful audience-ratings and these indicated the popularity of any kind of 'western'.

I think none of us then envisaged the TV plays of to-day: science-fiction; space-adventure, explicit-sex and violence; or the pernicious video horror films.

For sometime, Mr Kelly had been giving pupils more responsible participation on public occasions too, especially Speech Days.

The first innovation was when Maureen Howe, a Fourth Year pupil who had won First Prize in the Rotary Public Speaking Competition, prepared and presented the School Report, after Mr Kelly had spoken briefly to the guests. He said,

'In these days it is perhaps a natural thing to allow pupils to run their own show. The success of such a venture, of course, depends on the kind of teaching they receive.'

The occasion was reported in several newspapers including the *Daily Mail*, which carried the headline, "Headmistress for the Day."

"Maureen, 14, makes the school 'sit up' at her Speech Day."

In 1967 the pupils conducted Speech Day entirely on their own. Michael Ince, Head Boy, acting as Chairman, welcomed Mr Edward Milne MP and his wife, Governors, parents, and the Guest of Honour, Mr W Lynn, Chief Inspector of Schools for Northumberland.

The school reports on academic successes and school activities were given by senior girls, Ann Gray and Kathleen Dodds.

After Mr Lynn had addressed the assembly and presented the prizes, a vote of thanks was offered by Ann Farmborough.

Mr Lynn said afterwards how appreciative he was of the way in which the young people had conducted their own Speech Day.

Eventually, there came a Speech Day when the prizes were presented and the address given by an ex-pupil, a loyal supporter of the school over many years, who, by this time, was married with two children and worked as a Ward Sister at the RVI Newcastle upon Tyne.

In 1969, my husband and I began to think about retiring. We bought a caravette and felt we should like more time to travel and pursue our respective hobbies whilst still active enough to enjoy them.

Teaching was becoming more arduous and less fulfilling. The number of malcontents, eager to combat authority and exert a personal power, to the detriment of classroom ease and a good working atmosphere, was growing. Although still a small minority, they were attracting an increasing number of half-hearted followers. There were acts of senseless vandalism; petty thieving in school and in local shops, not for the sake of the goods stolen, but as an achievement of a subversive aim and a token of one-upmanship; graffiti appeared; books were surreptitiously damaged; to rouse a teacher's anger became a collective aim.

My relationship with most classes remained good, but, with some, I could no longer show friendly ease: it was necessary to be vigilant, firm, and outwardly at least, unperturbed.

In Religious Education sessions with senior year-groups in the hall, I could no longer sit at ease amongst them, reading and discussing: I stood on the platform so that I could locate and foil any attempts to disrupt.

One morning, I was suddenly aware, for the first time in almost forty years of teaching, how vulnerable and at the mercy of a class a teacher can be. Physically, almost anyone of those present had the ability to overcome me.

I finished the lesson, dismissed the group (about sixty in number) went into my empty classroom and sat down at my table, my eyes misted by tears. I was sad for this generation of teenagers, deprived of natural joy by the malaise of the times; sad for the school, whose friendly atmosphere was being dissipated by a fortuitous antagonism; sad for myself and my new uneasy awareness.

Next came news of structural changes due to be effected locally within a year or two, a realignment of age-groups involving amalgamation of pupils from various schools. There were to be First Schools for those aged five years to nine, Middle Schools for the nine to thirteen years group, and High Schools for those thirteen years old and upwards. Delaval was to be a Middle School. This made our retirement plans decisive.

I would not disrupt my Fifth Year by leaving before their CSE Examination which was scheduled for the end of April and the first week in May of 1970 so we submitted our resignations for 30th April.

31.

We should like to have left unobtrusively, just walking out together as usual on our last day, without official leave-taking or poignancy of farewell, but this was not possible as our posts had to be advertised, and my departure involved a considerable reorganization of classes and duties. Nevertheless, we said we wished to leave as unobtrusively as possible and insisted that no formal announcement be made to the children and no collection of money initiated to buy gifts.

Headmaster and Staff complied with this request, but the news of our departure, still some months ahead, inevitably became known. The result astonished and moved me, there was so much general concern. How were they going to manage without me? How was I going to manage without them? Who would people go to if they felt ill?

I said other teachers could meet their needs and I would leave the girls the 'coat'.

I had an old fur-fabric coat that had been at school for years and used originally when I umpired netball in cold weather.

One day, a girl felt sick and was in obvious pain and I wrapped the coat around her for comfort and warmth. After that, on odd occasions, would come the request, 'So-and-so isn't feeling well, Mrs Wrigley. May she wear the coat?'

I treasure the memory of those last months at Delaval. They could have been desolate and frustrating, an old teacher working out her last days, but, instead, they were rich and rewarding. The majority put effort into their work, and my Fifth Formers were marvellous. They were so friendly and affectionate; the classroom atmosphere was completely relaxed, the work they produced their best. Their anxiety was that I might be lonely in the years ahead without children to teach.

One boy went to a performance of a Townswomen's Guild pantomime, an entertainment quite alien to his normal taste. Next morning he came to tell me this, and concluded, 'So you go and do pantomimes for them when you leave. Your scripts are streets ahead of theirs.'

A biased opinion.

I produced my last pantomime in March, 1970, reviving for the occasion 'The Lost Totem'. Its theme was even more topical than when it was written sixteen years previously; the need for peace; for good relationships and mutual understanding.

As the week of the production drew nearer the general excitement increased and my feeling of tension deepened. I suppose I was less calm than usual. I wanted the last show to be as perfect as possible, yet rehearsals seemed difficult: principals would be absent, lines forgotten, groups not assembled at the appointed time, occasional overt attempts at disruption displayed.

Tickets sold rapidly and those for the last evening had to be rationed because the demand was so great. I seemed to go through the pantomime in my sleep.

The final rehearsal at Newlands did not go very well, but having checked that costumes, scenery, props and make-up were all in readiness there was no more I could do.

In the event, each evening went smoothly and well, and at last, it was almost time to open the curtains for the final performance. The hall was packed with parents and past scholars: the cast seethed with excitement as the National Anthem was played and the curtains opened.

I think every youngster played to the limit of his or her ability and stage hands and other helpers crowded round me in the wings, joining in the cowboy songs and 'Smoking the pipe of peace'.

As the curtains closed at the end of the performance more old pupils who had been unable to get tickets surged in at the back of the hall. The curtains opened for the players to make their final bow and someone drew me on to the stage. The applause from hall, stage and wings overwhelmed me. Someone made a speech and into my arms were put a beautiful bouquet and my green glass vase. It is here in the room as I write, filled with roses. It is pale green, translucent, faceted – and very dear to me.

That was one of the memorable moments of my life as a teacher: it was wonderful to be surrounded by so much affection.

Eventually the audience had gone; so many old friends had lingered to speak to me. The cast had eaten their Eskimo pies – icecream in biscuit cases, topped with chocolate, a speciality of a local ice-cream manufacturer. It had become customary to distribute these on the last night of every show.

Then we grouped the players for an assortment of photographs before the scenery was removed. It was late by the time willing helpers had packed costumes, found lost property, and almost everyone dispersed. Then there was silence, an empty hall, a stage bare except for the Totem on its pole and the six Fifth Form boys who had been scene-shifting. My husband photographed me standing among them beside the Totem.

Then good-nights were said, the lads went away, the caretaker came to put out the lights and we came home.

The last pantomime was over.

Masefield's line came into my mind 'Life's an affair of instants spun to years.'

The evening had been one such instant.

32.

On a Tuesday morning at the beginning of April, I was clearing cupboards, checking stock and removing sets of books to where they would be required, helped by a band of pupils. As I was walking out of my classroom, followed by boys with armfuls of books, a *Blyth News* reporter arrived to interview me about my pending departure. I explained that we did not want publicity, but she said that a husband and wife teaching in the same school for more than twenty years was newsworthy and mention would be made of it whether we were interviewed or not.

One of the boys behind me interpolated, 'Go on, miss, talk to her. You might be on the telly.'

I said to her, 'It is obviously inconvenient for me to talk to you at the moment, but we have holiday on Thursday, so if you would care to come to our home and have coffee with us we'll have a chat.' (I think it must have been a local election day.)

She duly arrived on the Thursday morning accompanied by a photographer. Lewis and I were photographed in our front garden. Then we sat by the fire having coffee and talking.

On 16th April there was a three-column spread on the front page of the *Blyth News*, boldly titled.

"COUPLE RETIRING AFTER TEACHING 28 YEARS AT THE SAME SCHOOL,"

and including a six inches by four picture of us.

Next morning, there was an obvious display of copies of the newspaper and numerous comments were offered.

One junior girl said dolefully, 'Our dog ate you last night, Miss, and I couldn't get another paper.'

During ensuing weeks letters and cards arrived from near and far from past pupils reviving memories and wishing us well.

As 30th April drew nearer, I told inquiring pupils that we were not going to leave properly on that date, as we would be in and out of school on several days the following week and would say goodbye to everyone after that.

We offered the little Fifth Form a day out with us the week after their examinations were completed, and suggested a trip to the Farne Islands, a visit to a show in Newcastle or a party at our home. They debated briefly among themselves and then the spokesman said, 'We'll come to the Wrigley pad.' And so it was agreed.

We arranged for the delivery at school, on the first Friday in May, of sufficient Eskimo pies and small bottles of 'pop' to supply everyone and we went ourselves about two o'clock to arrange for its distribution in each classroom by the Fifth Formers, just before playtime, after which Mr Kelly was allowing the pupils to go home early, leaving the Staff free to join us in a small celebration.

The ice-cream and mineral water were a welcome surprise to the recipients, but lovely surprises awaited us too. For instance, flowers! Our house was like a bower for a week. There were bunches, sprays and bouquets from groups and individuals, from pupils past and present, including a bunch of red roses from a mother and daughter, both of whom I had taught, the mother at Princess Louise School in 1935, the daughter at Delaval; and a bouquet of spring flowers tied with green and mauve ribbons, the colours I most frequently wore, from three sisters, by then past scholars, Margaret, Marion and Ann Douglass.

The Fifth Form had waiting for us a framed reproduction of Constable's *Hay Wain* accompanied by two Gordon Crier cards signed by each of them. Mine depicted a woman, wearing a big sunhat, lying in a hammock surrounded by flowers, with a little brown dog at her feet. (They had sometimes met me walking in the woods with Dandy, my brother's brown poodle.) On Lewis' card was a man sitting on a motor-mower reading a gardening book and having a drink.

Everywhere we went there were cards and gifts, such an assortment, and obviously spontaneously chosen. There were vases, a coffee pot, a decanter, jam dishes, ash-trays, butter dishes, (including the one we use every day still which has a cow on the lid for a handle) two miniature 'greenhouses' for cuttings, stacks of plant pots, and pillowcases. There was an embroidered tablecloth from the caretaker and his wife.

The giving and receiving, and the eating and drinking, as we moved fairly quickly from room to room, made it a joyful occasion, no time given to laments or sadness.

Afterwards, when we went up to the Staff room another pleasant surprise awaited us – Mr Soulsby was among the friends assembled there.

We knew we were to receive a gift from the Staff; it would have been a falsity to try to prevent it, and it was a delightful one, a complete Royal Doulton tea service in the Pastoral design, fine white china, silver-rimmed, with a spray of small flowers in pastel shades on each side. We both appreciated it very much and it has had frequent use without a breakage, because I always handle it with great care. Only the teapot is rarely used as I am afraid I might knock the spout off as I empty it and wash it. I am rather clumsy in that way.

Farewells were eventually completed, and as we drove away from school for the last time, the car laden with flowers and gifts, some pupils still lingered to wave us on our way.

The elation lingered on when we reached home. Arranging the flowers, displaying the gifts, preoccupied me. We had preparations to make for two parties, the Fifth Form party and a friendly, informal evening for colleagues past and present. I spent hours in the kitchen baking and preparing whilst Lewis shifted furniture around and arranged liquid refreshment. We felt on holiday, not as if our teaching days were over.

The Fifth Form arrived after school the following Wednesday, all smart and smiling, some carrying records. They roamed around the garden and took photographs, then chatted away as they did justice to a buffet meal in the dining-room. Afterwards, they played records and danced in the hall or went up to the loft to play snooker.

Then they all gathered around the fire and talked until it was time to go. The girls insisted on washing the dishes, after which they collected their records, said goodbye and thanks and went home.

The Staff party was later the same week.

It was not until the following Monday morning that the truth really dawned: I was not going to school as a teacher anymore! I walked through the woods to the field by the river. There were no children playing; there was no one there except me and the brown poodle, Dandy. A sense of remorse overwhelmed me: I suddenly felt as if I had buried my one talent.

But this feeling soon passed over ensuing weeks, and I discovered that, although we were no longer teaching, our relationship with Delaval remained.

A group of cross-country runners out practising would call in passing.

A few who had gone on to Ashington Technical College came to borrow books or seek help with Literature.

Some kept in regular contact, others called spasmodically over the years. The post brought Christmas cards, Easter cards, letters from far-away places, packages of wedding cake and photographs of babies. We went to one or two weddings, including that of Pauline Newton, the first of that final Fifth Form to marry.

Shopping in Blyth was almost a social round, as shop assistants greeted us. I remember my embarrassment one morning when a greengrocery assistant saw me, abandoned the other customers and insisted on examining each box in a pile to find the one containing the best strawberries. One girl was in a post office, two in banks, and one was the first woman bus driver in the area.

We were served petrol by past pupils and had our dustbin emptied by one. They came as house decorators, electricians, and employees of building contractors. A police dog-handler, Billy Smith, used to come with Tara to see us after he had finished a training session with her in a nearby field.

In retirement the pace of life slows. You don't work to a timetable and can forget the date of the year and almost the day of the week. You have time to be completely absorbed in a project and time to be luxuriously idle. For almost ten years we enjoyed our various pursuits, enjoyed our homelife, travelled when we felt like it in the caravette. In 1976, we flew to Corfu, hired a motor-bike and explored the hill villages where women sat on doorsteps knitting shawls, men sat drinking wine outside tavernas and youngsters fetched water from wells in oil drums and jars, loaded on a donkey. We found wild cyclamen growing in olive groves, picked walnuts, and lemons. That year also we acquired our Border terrier, Kim.

In 1979 we worked a narrowboat for two from Penkbridge to Stourport and back along the Staffordshire canal.

In December 1980, my husband went into hospital for major surgery. He died of cancer in October, 1981.

In the sad final weeks of his terminal illness, we were bolstered by the compassionate and unremitting help of our families and of close friends of many years standing. We were aided also in practical ways by past pupils over the two final years of ill health. Keith Chamberlain, a motor engineer, who had helped Lewis to build a Rochdale sports car in 1969 looked after the car. Johnny Brooks, husband of Mavis Watson who had been Headgirl at the time of Mr Soulsby's retirement, did any jobs required manual strength and heavy lifting. And there were others.

Immediately after the death announcement appeared in local newspapers I received phone calls and visits from past pupils. Then came cards and letters, (so many containing the word 'respect'), and a beautiful bunch of chrysanthemums tied with mauve and green ribbons from the three sisters, Margaret, Marion and Ann Douglass.

I felt proud and humble for us both at the funeral. The little chapel was filled to overflowing, mourners extending into the corridor. There was no organ but the hymn was started, as arranged, by the rich true voice of Margaret Haley (at that time still teaching at Delaval) and then the place was filled with the sound of 'The day thou gavest Lord is ended'.

As I walked out with my brother into the October sunlight, they came one by one to greet me, Staff and pupils and some parents, ranging the years from 1942 to 1970. It was memorable, emotional, sadly beautiful and strangely comforting.

33.

We had been married for forty-two years all but a week; we had shared our days both in work and leisure, and now I was alone in our home, except for our Border terrier, Kim.

I shall always be immensely grateful for the affection, solicitude and practical help given continuously by my immediate family and longstanding friends, but detail of these is irrelevant here, because this is the story of Delaval. I have received manifold repayment in practical help and in friendship for anything I may have contributed to the good of the school. For instance, Keith Chamberlain came and saw to the selling of the car (It was pointless to keep it as I am unable to drive). He sorted and tidied the accumulation of a lifetime in the garage.

I had thought that my evenings at symphony concerts, one of the great enjoyments of our married life, would be over, because of transport difficulties, but Keith's wife, Irene, enjoys the same type of music and suggested we went together. So she became a member of the Northern Sinfonia Society too and provides transport and congenial company for all the concerts.

Erstwhile colleague, Jeff Crozier, and his wife Elsie, whom I taught at Princess Louise Road School, welcome me to their family circle. I am 'auntie' to their three children, now adults, who visit me in friendship and are willing to undertake any practical jobs around the house or garden which are beyond my strength or skill.

Mavis and Johnny Brooks visit me regularly and I can rely on him for any jobs requiring physical strength. He has just renewed windows in the greenhouse broken by gale force winds.

As a member of a Townswomen's Guild, Mavis invited me in November to their annual social evening, which comprises a sale of work, some form of entertainment and supper. The first to greet me as I began to look around the stalls was Mrs Douglass (a different Douglass from the three sisters mentioned previously). We had taught all her sons and daughters and after the last one left she wrote to thank us for the quality of teaching they had received. She came to my husband's funeral. She is a widow too, petite and serene, always smartly dressed in clothes made by Edna, one of her daughters, who, on leaving school, went to train as a dressmaker at a good fashion house in the region. She had always shown special aptitude at Needlework.

When I sat down to supper I found I had taught everyone else at the table, and there was more talking than eating, as they told me their news. One of them, Dorothy Warwick, had married a Delaval boy, and I had taught their children too. One of them, John had gone into ordnance surveying. He joined the RAF, crewed one leg (USA to Bermuda) in the RAF yacht taking part in the Trans-Atlantic Race, and later became a cartographer in Persia.

Mavis' Aunt Margaret, also an old girl was another. She is a wholesale buyer with a business of her own.

I meet Elizabeth Harrison, one of a large Delaval family, out with her children or her dog, or both. She visits me and gives me news of the others. Her mother was a keen gardener and I still have descendants of a gloxinia she gave us many years ago.

Jacqueline Hudson née Simm came to take me to have tea with her and her family when she moved to a new bungalow recently.

One day, as I was weeding the front garden, a passer-by paused, recognised me, and came in to introduce her two daughters to her old teacher.

Another woman walked through the woods with me, last year, when I met her with some children. She is a past pupil who has had a hard life herself, but does valiant youth work with deprived children.

Last October I was invited to the At Home of the Mayoress of Blyth Valley. The Mayor was Gilbert Barker, longtime governor and friend of Delaval School, and his wife Norma, also a past-pupil.

Two press photographers were in attendance. Ian Woodhouse from the *Newcastle Journal* and David Webb representing the *Blyth News*, both old scholars of Delaval. David Webb is now the *Newcastle Evening Journal* photographer and picture editor.

As I joined the queue of people waiting to be received by the Mayor and Mayoress, the guest nearest me said, 'Do you remember me? You used to teach me many years ago.' (She is now the wife of a Headmaster.)

Someone in front looked round and said, 'You taught me too. I was Ellen Farmer.'

SMILER REMEMBERS

Once inside, and seated at a table in a corner having afternoon tea, friends began to gather round, beginning with Mrs Douglass, two of her daughters and a grand-daughter and members of the Bolam family who had been staunch members of the Old Scholars Drama Club. Eventually, there were so many of us that someone said, if there had been a netball court there, we had enough past team-players to have a game.

They all had news to give of their progress in life and their families and there was much happy reminiscing amongst them. I came away with cordial invitations and with promises to call and see me.

Christmas brought its usual spate of cards and letters from near and far.

One from Jean Walton told me her son had gained an Honours Degree in Business Studies and was now working. She visits me sometimes, and writes at Christmas and Easter.

Kathleen Soulsby enclosed a photograph of her fourteen-month-old son Keith who 'is a bundle of laughs. He is walking and into everything. It is amazing how much he understands.'

A Christmas has never passed since I first taught them without cards from Kathleen and her friend, Pauline Newton. Sandra Mapp (née Heron) encloses news of her family.

There is always one from Ivan Barrass and from Jack Saddler who joined the Navy as a wireless operator about 1950 and later went to work at Cranwell. He called to see me recently, accompanied by his wife. He is now retired.

During the past month, I have had three typical visitors.

One arrived one afternoon on his motor-bike to chat over a cup of tea and leave Alexei Tolstoy's Trilogy *Ordeal* for me to read. A few years ago his offering was the autobiography of Karl Marx and I insisted on him borrowing reciprocally my copy of Solzhenitsyn's *Gulag Archipelago*.

We recommended him in 1961 for the 13+ Examination which he passed. He was transferred to the Grammar School and thence to Manchester University where he gained a BSc degree.

One morning I received a phone call from Tom Wilcox who said he had been away from the locality for twenty-four years, but was back visiting his parents, had found my number in the telephone directory and would like to come and see me one evening for an hour. He came that evening and it was eleven o'clock when he went away: there had been so many incidents and personalities to recall.

SMILER REMEMBERS

On leaving Delaval, he had gone to Ashington Technical College, gained good proficiency certificates and eventually arrived at Yeovil where he is an engineer inspector at Westlands.

He smiled and commented his way through the Delaval Scrapbook where his name appears as the 'coconut shy man' in the cast of the 'Magic Carpet'.

He has a son in engineering and a daughter training to be a teacher.

Ann Charlton, née Wardle, Sultana in the 'Magic Carpet' and a principal in other pantomimes emigrated, after her marriage, to Toronto, where she was, for eighteen years, an investment counsellor, and works now on the educational side of the Investment Dealers' Association of Canada. She celebrated her silver wedding in 1979 and has a nineteen-year-old son.

Last week, she came back to visit her mother, and came to spend an evening with me. She is a happy fulfilled woman with firmness of character and a good outlook.

As she recalled schooldays long gone, she said, 'I have never heard anyone say a word against New Delaval School.'

She invited me to visit her in Toronto.

She sometimes visits an old friend who lives near Ottawa, Theresa Davies, née McCallan, who became a nursing sister in the Queen Alexandra Nursing Service and was working as a sister at the Royal Victoria Hospital in Newcastle when she came to present the prizes at New Delaval Speech Day.

In the spring this year, one of her English nursing friends made a ciné film to send to her. She came here one afternoon when I was gardening, told me about the film, and said her husband was about to complete it if I would go into the house, answer the door when she rang the bell, then come out and walk down the drive to the gate with her. She insisted I appear just as I was, dishevelled, in gardening trousers and top.

Subsequently, there came a long letter from Theresa from which I shall quote briefly: 'It was so nice to receive the lovely movie that Dorothy sent out of you and my family. Mind, you haven't changed, even though your hair is white. You are still the attractive lady I'll always remember. Some evenings, just sitting, I'll watch it with such fond memories.

My girls can't understand that their mother would be sitting writing to her teacher and with such fond memories. They really can't understand while I watch you on the movie that I shed a few tears. It is quite beyond their comprehension.'

Another letter I shall always treasure came from one of my last Fifth Formers, David Wilson, 'Wilsa'; 'King of the School', the teenager who made me the wooden bowl as a leaving present.

He is happily married to an Australian girl, Jenny, and has two daughters, Cherie and Melanie, whom he loves dearly. He wrote to me from Dee Why in New South Wales where he now lives.

Here is an extract:

> I often talk to Jenny of my days at Delaval, of the pantomimes and other good times; they were good and made even more so by the great teachers we had.
>
> I was very sorry and saddened to hear of your sad loss. All I can say is that you both were so lucky to have each other and you shared more in your lives than most other couples would have in six lives; of that you can be proud.
>
> Sydney is a beautiful city and I rate it one of the most colourful in the world. The harbour and Pacific are just so blue it seems the colours on the post cards and pictures one sees are lacking true colour. We are living about five minutes away from a two-mile stretch of beach, with lagoons on the other side stretching right out to Palm Beach.
>
> If you get the chance to jump on a plane, don't miss it. You would be made most welcome to stay with us. That is if you can get Kim 'baby-sat' for a few months.

The mode of education and the building in which it takes place are not the first essentials: what matters most is knowing and caring about the children you try to teach, not providing all with the same opportunities, but rather devising a curriculum suited to the needs of each individual, so that each occupies a place in society where she or he can have a sense of personal completeness, doing work suited to their own particular aptitudes. It is essential to help every individual to be aware of natural joy too, joy of sound and movement; fragrance and colour, form and texture, in the living world around them. I would try to show everyone that material possessions, social élitism and contrived pursuits are subsidiary to spiritual awareness and the joy of the natural world. Let them look for a blade of grass in the city turmoil, listen for a bird's song in the metropolis and turn off the transistor long enough to learn that silence is beautiful, not frightening, that awareness of eternity is possible in the silence of space.

These were our aims at Delaval Secondary Modern School.

Quite a number of Delaval pupils went on to take University degrees, including recently the Open University. Michael Jaggs, a member of the last Fifth Form (1970) gained a First Class Honours Degree in Engineering in 1982. Just as important, basically, a mongol boy left school twenty-odd years ago to become a road sweeper and he is a *good* road-sweeper, with pride in the appearance of the place.

I cannot enumerate all the walks of life into which Delaval pupils have gone: There have been many nurses, shop assistants, skilled artisans, factory-workers, civil service workers and typists.

Joyce Mitcheson left Delaval at fourteen and a half years of age and progressed to Skerry's College in Newcastle, where, at fifteen, she was star pupil in a demonstration at which she took down 200 words a minute in shorthand, then read back her script to the audience. She was also one of ten typists who typed to music at speeds up to 100 words a minute. At school, she had an aptitude for writing poems and short stories.

One boy became a non-conformist minister and married a fellow-pupil. One girl became an income tax clerk and a local preacher, another is a vicar's wife. Some have built up businesses of their own as butcher, electrician, blacksmith, engineer, painter and decorator. There are several policemen, a fireman, numerous motor-mechanics and gardeners. There are dentists' and doctors' receptionists. There are chefs (in hotels and on a liner) and a confectioner, Cyril Ward, who helped to make Princess Margaret's wedding cake when he was assistant to the champion confectioner, Mr D R Adams of Morecambe.

One girl who, in her Final year, chose to do Woodwork and Technical Drawing, instead of Domestic Science, later worked in the drawing-office of a Tyne shipyard. One boy, Joe Fullerton, became apprentice of the year there.

There are several insurance agents, an insurance broker, two managers of super-markets and an area-supervisor for Woolworth's.

George Kennedy is head of a catering consortium and his work entails travel in Africa and the Middle East.

One girl left to be nursemaid to a family in London. When the children no longer needed her she became nurse-companion to their grandmother with whom she travelled in Europe, lived in Switzerland, and was treated like a daughter.

Once I received a parcel from Palestine containing two embroidered cushion-covers. A young soldier serving out there had been reminded by place names of Religious Education lessons at school and had sent the present as a memento.

186

Robin Barker, son of Gilbert Barker, and Boy Dodger in 'The Lost Totem' is head of a comprehensive school in Lancashire.

There are teachers, colliery draughtsmen and computer operators.

Successes enumerated are not achievements because of the type of work done, but rather that in those tasks they are satisfactorily attuned to life. They maintain a loyalty to and respect for their place of education.

It matters that a young man of Delaval, Peter Barningham, brought his fiancée, later his wife, then his baby daughter to see my husband and me. He did not come again until this year when he came to tell me that his wife had given birth to a son that morning, and he grieved because Lewis was not here to learn the glad tidings too.

Epilogue

I reached this point of recall eight years ago, having spent leisure hours for two years happily writing. Then like farmers' fields my book was set aside.

But soon it is to be published, so the final words must be written.

The world is now a sadder place where lethal violence, deprivation, alienation, crime and AIDS flourish.

Last week I saw on Tyne and Tees Television the return home of an eleven year old boy who had been convicted that day, not for the first time, of stealing and driving away a car although he was too small to see over the driving wheel.

He strutted forward, a short hooded figure to receive a hero's welcome from his mates, all hooded or with heads wrapped in scarves, gesturing derisively at the cameras.

The only adult in sight was an unrelated man offering comments over his garden gate. Where were the parents? Where were the fathers? Men who should have been exerting control, winning respect, acting as role models.

How many youngsters are offsprings of casual promiscuity doomed to a life of domestic instability, free to play truant, to steal and vandalise, with before them only the prospect of insecure relationships and unemployment. The fabric of family life seems warped and torn, yet there are threads of hope.

There must be other unobtrusive communities like Delaval where schools have provided durable standards of education and families where stability survives over generations.

I am eighty-three years old, so some of my past pupils are senior citizens too. I meet them shopping, or walking in the woods and they pause to talk nostalgically of their school days. One greeted me affectionately as we waited in the Post Office to draw our pensions.

Middle-aged ones meet me or visit me and talk about their grown up children.

I met Derek McSparron in the woods one day and heard about his son who is an instrument technician and his daughter at Glasgow University. He married fellow pupil Caroline Self and they have celebrated their Silver Wedding. He works at Alcan but still keeps up his interest in Art for which he showed special aptitude at school. There was an exhibition of his paintings in Bedlington recently.

Jean Watson, née Reid, wrote to say her daughter Alison had gained a BA Honours degree.

George Wilson had leisure to visit me because he has retired from being leader of the North-East Mine Rescue Team.

Last week my dog went out to greet the friendly men who empty the dustbins. One said

'We are introducing her to the new man, Maurice Dobson. You used to teach his father and he drives the wagon.'

I went to the gate to speak to Henry and he told me of classmates he had met recently.

John Prior, manager of a Presto supermarket, called me in passing.

A car pulled up beside me one morning and out stepped a portly smiling man, Frank Jackson, now site-manager for a building firm. I recalled him as the agile mischievous monkey in 'Another Sleeping Beauty'.

John Howe who left school in 1954 called yesterday for coffee and a chat on his way home from a cycle ride in the country. He helps to run a farm shop and is an amateur naturalist with a growing collection of butterflies.

Today Colin Gaskell brought me a tape recording of Russian opera and we talked of books, travel and mineralogy.

Christmas is not long past and it brought the usual heart warming cards, letters and gifts.

For dessert tonight I ate the last of the mandarins in cointreau brought by Mavis Brooks. Last year I attended her daughter's wedding.

Yesterday I made the last mince pies of the festive season, emptying the jar of mince brought by Jacqueline Hudson, née Simm, along with a Christmas pudding and flowers. Her daughter Zelda is training to be a nurse.

Last night I went with Irene Chamberlain to the Northern Sinfonia Orchestra's performance of Fauré's *Requiem*. Her husband Keith, who left Delaval in 1956, has just been promoted Senior Technical Officer at the Northumbria Police Vehicle Repairs Workshops.

Kathleen Patterson, née Soulsby, happily married with three children, wanted to work with children when her own went to school so she trained to be a play group leader with the Play Group Association and gained their diploma, DPP. She also acts as a co-tutor in high schools on North Tyneside doing basic foundation work with fifteen year olds doing child development courses. I quote from her recent letter

> 'From September to Christmas I was working at the Meadowell Playgroup. The estate is a mass of boarded up houses, some of which are still lived in.
> 'The children were rather a handful at first, but as they got to know me and I them, their attitude changed towards me and the other members of the team.'

So the future does hold hope.

Choosing a title for my memoirs presents no problem. All teachers have nicknames. I probably had many over the years. I believe I latterly was known as Gladys, because I rather flogged the story of *The Small Woman* by Gladys Aylward. But a past pupil told me that her mother had been a pupil at New Delaval School when I first went there and they had named me 'Smiler' and that I was 'Smiler' to her generation too.

So with love and gratitude to every pupil I ever taught I dedicate *Smiler Remembers*.